T0121674

Order this book online at www.trafford.com
or email orders@trafford.com

Most Trafford titles are also available at major online book retailers.

© Copyright 2009 James Starnes.
All rights reserved. No part of this publication may be reproduced, stored in a retrieval system, or
transmitted, in any form or by any means, electronic, mechanical, photocopying, recording, or
otherwise, without the written prior permission of the author.

Note for Librarians: A cataloguing record for this book is available from Library
and Archives Canada at www.collectionscanada.ca/amicus/index-e.html

Printed in Victoria, BC, Canada.

ISBN: 978-1-4251-9045-3

*Our mission is to efficiently provide the world's finest, most comprehensive book publishing
service, enabling every author to experience success. To find out how to publish your book, your
way, and have it available worldwide, visit us online at www.trafford.com*

Trafford rev. 09/11/09

North America & international
toll-free: 1 888 232 4444 (USA & Canada)
phone: 250 383 6864 ♦ fax: 812 355 4082

The Cross at Beautiful Lake Junaluska, N.C.

Stories by Rev. James A. Starnes
Prayers by Mrs. Myrtle M. Starnes
Cover Photo by Rev. Norwood Montgomery

Dedication
To
Myrtle Amelia McNeill Starnes

This book is dedicated to my dear wife;
who, for over 50 years, has been the joy of my life.
She is the sweetest person I have ever known.
And amazingly, over the years our love has grown.

She has been the perfect mother;
    Our children would have chosen no other.
She is my heart and my life;
    My wonderful friend; my beautiful wife.

She is the steady hand within my life's glove;
I thank the Good Lord for her supportive love.

I know 'God-Jesus-Holy Spirit' enjoys her prayers;
For when she prays for others, she sincerely cares.

Thank you my darling wife, lover and friend.
You are indeed, what I need... a God send. Amen.

ON THE JOY OF LIVING
THE FAITH

Me and Mrs. Poor have been serving the good Lord for nigh onto fifty years now. Through the hard times and the glad, we have experienced God's blessings and His abundant life in Jesus Christ.

During our marriage, it has been our opportunity to "pastor" some twenty small rural churches, usually two or three at a time. We hope you will enjoy these stories that we have collected over the years. May some of them inspire and encourage you to live the faith and to share the joy.

Me and Mrs. Poor believe in the "Love principle" Jesus taught and embodied. More, we believe in and commune with the Spirit Jesus called "Abba." We believe you too can experience an awareness of this Spirit (as Creator-creating God) by praying and meditating.

If you ain't one yet, may you become an Easter person. *God bless, Brother and Mrs. Poor*

1

***Prayer by Mrs. Poor**: Dear Lord, if it is in Your will, please put Your blessings on this book and use it to Your glory. May all the stories point the readers toward Jesus and His teachings about love. Amen.*

ARE YOU PREPARED?

A man with a weak heart inherited $500,000. His wife asked the reverend to tell him as tactfully as he could. Well, the reverend visited the man with the weak heart and talked about the weather, sports, and most of the news he could think of.

Then he asked, "John, what would you do if someone gave you $500,000.00?"

"No question about it," the man with the weak heart said. "I'd give half of it to the church."

When he heard that, the preacher with the good heart fell over dead! Sooner or later, brothers and sisters, we're gonna each one fall over dead. Are you prepared?

See you in church,   *Brother Poor*

***Prayer by Mrs. Poor**: Dear Lord, may we become smart enough to be prepared for death. May we have the insight to consult with a pastor to make sure we understand God's plan for salvation. Amen.*

AND THE RAINS CAME DOWN

Man, did it rain the other night. Thunder and lightening — Wow! God was really proving His power. Reminded me of the time a little fellow named Johnny woke up in the middle of the night frightened 'cause of a storm. He was so skeered, he ran into his momma and daddy's room and asked if he could stay. His dad said that would be fine, but there really wasn't no need to be afraid 'cause Jesus was in that room with him.

The young fellow said he knew that; but if it was all the same, he wanted somebody in the room with skin on 'em.

Well, let me tell you, brothers and sisters — I know what little Johnny meant. There are times when we need somebody with "skin on 'em" to talk to — or to hear us — or to lean on. If you've been there, you also know what little Johnny means.

On the other hand, it's our Christian duty to put some skin around the principles of love and truth and beauty so that others might see Christ in us. How 'bout it? Do you walk it like you talk it?

See you in church.

Brother Poor

Prayer by Mrs. Poor:

Dear Lord,
May others see in our witness that You are the Savior of our soul, the Master of our mind, and the Lord of our life! Amen.

THE SLEEPING DEACON

I've been worrying about one of my deacons here lately. Seems every time I start preaching, he starts meditating — or at least he slowly closes his eyes and lowers his head.

When I asked him about it, he said he was paying me a compliment. I said, "What do you mean — a compliment?" He said, "Well, if one of them young preachers was up there speaking or one of them big city preachers, I'd have to stay awake and check out what they were saying. But I've come to trust you, Brother Poor. Don't you see, it's a compliment when I can trust a man enough to sleep while he's preaching."

And just when I thought I'd heard 'em all! We sure can come up with some dandy excuses, can't we, brothers and sisters? Know what the first excuse was that man ever used? According to our Bible, God asked Adam if he'd been eating them apples, and you remember what Adam said? Look up Genesis 3:12, and if you keep reading, you'll see it didn't take Eve long to think up one too.

Well, back to my problem with my "meditating deacon" and his excuse — for I've been thinking about it quite a bit. Seems to me it's sorta like my snoring at night. Mrs. Poor punches me and says, "Turn over, I. R., your snoring is gonna wake up the neighbors!" But I tell her my snoring ain't the problem — the problem is she's too light a sleeper. If she was a heavier sleeper, she wouldn't be hearing me no how.

I declare! I believe I just got the answer. The bottom line has to be: If I can't preach good enough to keep my deacons awake, they don't have a problem — I do.

So long, folks. I gotta go. I'm going over to the church now and practice my sermon to them empty pews and get me ready for Sunday. Brother Layman ain't gonna sleep this coming Lord's day. Hallelujah! Amen!

Brother Poor

Prayer by Mrs. Poor:

Wake us up, Lord; wake us up! Amen

IT TAKES MORE THAN SINGING AND SHOUTING

Three teenagers were on their way to a Halloween party, complete with costumes. One of the fellows was dressed like a devil — red suit, horns, tail and pitchfork. As they drove past a church where some of the members had gathered for choir practice, they got a wild idea . . . "Let's scare 'em!"

One of the teenagers turned off the lights while the other shined a flashlight on the "devil" as he ran down the aisle toward the choir loft.

They tell me that everybody ran — that is, except this rather fat lady who seemed to be too excited to run. She just stood there shaking.

Finally, she blurted out, "Mr. Devil! Please, Mr. Devil! I've been doing a lot of singing and a lot of shouting, but I've been on your side all the time."

Do you get the message, my fellow Christians? It takes more than singing and shouting. It takes sharing and service and salvation. *Brother Poor*

Prayer by Mrs. Poor:

Dear Lord:

Enable us to be on the side of love, truth, and beauty — as these elements culminate in the Christ. Amen.

GOD'S LIBRARY

The Bible is not just a book. It is not even just a Holy book. Rather, it is a library of 66 Holy books.

Books containing poetry, proverbs, words of hymns, recorded prayers, parables, letters, family genealogies, primitive legends passed down from generation to generation orally and then finally recorded, dreams, sermons, accounts of miracles, wars, and directions on how to get to heaven.

To me, it is the most important book ever written. I would rather have a familiarity with the books of the Bible than a Ph.D. Through the Bible, our God has spoken to me many times.

The Bible is not only a collection of books written by men seeking a God; the Holy Bible is a library of books through which God is seeking men and women. It is through the Bible that God and men have met, can meet, and will continue to meet.

The Bible is the inspired words of God, but it is inspiring to us only to the degree that we read it and study it and act on its advice. Mostly, I read the Bible to learn how the people of the book have faced similar problems that I am facing, how they discovered God's will for their journey, and how I can do the same.

My favorite verses in the entire Bible are Matthew 22:36-40 and I John 4:7-21. The longest chapter in the Bible is Psalm 119; the shortest and middle chapter is Psalm 117. The longest name in the Bible is in the 8th chapter of Isaiah (look it up and count the letters). The longest verse is Esther 8:9 (also you might be surprised if you count the number of times the name God is found in the book of Esther). The shortest verse is John 11:35. All the letters of the alphabet are in Ezra 7:11 except two. Can you find the missing letters?

I think the most important advice ever given about the Bible was written by Paul to his young friend Timothy . . . II Timothy 3:16-17. Folks, I sincerely believe the answers to life's important questions are in the Bible.   *Brother Poor*

Prayer by Mrs. Poor: *O, God, our Guide, Help us to realize that, just like we would get lost if we didn't read the road map, the Bible is our spiritual road map. May we read it and heed it. Amen.*

GOOD NEIGHBORS

A preacher does a lot of moving. Usually we get a call from a bigger church. You know the old joke: the Rev. tells the Mrs. to start packing while he goes over to the church and prays about it.

One time, we moved into a parsonage beside a woman who said now she felt pretty safe. A highway patrolman lived on one side and a preacher on the other.

Then a psychologist moved across the street from her, and this was too much. This is what she said, "Every time I walk across my yard, I don't know whether I'm going to be preached at, arrested, or psychoanalyzed!" Well, she was a good neighbor, and she really seemed to enjoy all three of us. But isn't this what we are called to do in life — put together the elements of law and love and intelligence. We all need preachers and policemen and professors working together to make this a better world. And these preachers and policemen and professors need your support. Think of that the next time you have roast preacher for dinner, or a policeman stops you for speeding, or your daughter brings home a "D" in arithmetic. Amen.

See you in church. *Brother Poor*

Prayer by Mrs. Poor:

Dear Lord,

Help us to live together better as brothers and sisters of the earth. Amen.

There's no Ice Cream
in Hell

We had an Ice Cream Social and a Special Singing at our church last Sunday night. Would you believe our little church ate 15 churns of that good ole homemade ice cream! And then after all the fun of visiting and eating, we listened to some great singing while we let the ice cream that we had just eaten melt. To me, the onliest thing better than eating lots of good ole ice cream is eating lots of ice cream while visiting with friends and listening to good singing. Man, did we have a wonderful time.

But would you believe the next day I heard some comments like these: "Huh, if you have to feed 'em to get 'em to church, there must not be much to 'em."

And . . . "Some of these people better get to reading their Bibles 'cause there won't be no ice cream in hell."

Now isn't it a shame that some people can't seem to enjoy life. They have to complain and fuss and criticize 'bout any and everything. I just can't stand to be around such people. They'd just about make even ole St. Paul lose all his religion.

Life is so short. Let's count our blessings and rejoice. Christ came that we might have life, and that we might have it more abundantly. If heaven don't have no joy and laughter and singing, then I don't really want to go.

How can anyone get up at daybreak and meditate; or hug a child; or taste a squash casserole, some green beans seasoned with fatback, or some delicious ice cream; watch a glorious sunset; or listen to a gospel quartet sing of God's unconditional love, without rejoicing and praising God. Let those who will, complain; but as far as I'm concerned, they have a problem that prevents them from enjoying the gifts and blessings of Almighty God.

When you look for good things as a Christian should, you are going to find good things to talk and sing about. Brothers and sisters of the faith, enjoy the church of your choice regularly. And don't let the complainers bring you down to their level. See ya in church.   *Brother Poor*

Prayer by Mrs. Poor:

Thanks, dear God, for the abundant life. Amen.

THANKS-LIVING

Every time I get a little ahead, something happens and I wind up behind again. The insurance goes up, the car won't crank, my kid gets sick and there's doctor bills and medicines, my wife wants a new dress, or I see something real important that we need — like a new fishing rod.

Looks like I'm never gonna get rich. But then, there's the other side of the coin — I am rich!

Why, Land of Gracious, the other day I visited one of my members in the Dukes Hospital. He was facing surgery, so we had a prayer and asked the good Lord to guide the hands of the physician. On my way out of the hospital, I stopped in to speak with some of the other patients on the same floor — amputees, nervous conditions, cancer, very sick people facing major surgeries, etc.

14

Then on my way back home, I saw a red light flashing down the road. I thought, "Hope nobody is hurt bad!" Sure enough, there had been a wreck. The rescue squad was placing a badly injured woman in their truck. Some family was about to receive a heartbreaking message.

When I got back to the parsonage, my beloved had supper ready. Me and her and the kids sat down to eat. We all bowed our heads and I said this grace:

"Thank you, God, for all our blessings — for I am indeed a rich man. Amen."

Brothers and Sisters of the faith, may we count our many blessings that we so often take for granted.

See you in church.   *Brother Poor*

Prayer by Mrs. Poor:

Thank you, dear Lord, for all our blessings. Amen.

He Died for You

Let me tell you a story 'bout two soldiers who were under enemy fire. One got wounded and was lying out there in no-man's land calling for help. His buddy crawled out of his foxhole and went out and brought his friend back. But just as he reached the safety of the shelter, a bullet pierced his neck and killed him instantly. He saved his buddy, but it cost him his life.

A couple years later, the boy's father, with a "purple heart," went to meet the now-discharged soldier who his son had saved. To his surprise, the father found the boy drunk, and insultingly rude. He was unemployed, uneducated, and uncommitted to the Christian faith.

The father said to him, "Look here, young man, my son died for you and I expect better out of you. In like manner, Almighty God says to a world with way too many unemployed, undereducated, and uncommitted . . . "My Son died for you!"

See you in church!   *Brother Poor*

Prayer by Mrs. Poor:

Dear Lord,

Help us to become the best person we can be and thereby help make this a better world. Amen.

Too Quick on the Trigger

The other day, Ray Ivey took a friend of his bird hunting over on J. D.'s place. Of course, he had permission; but just to be on the neighborly side, he asked his 'huntin' buddy to wait in the truck while he said "Howdy" to J. D. His neighbor said, "No problem — anytime." But then he asked a favor of Ray. Seems he had an old mule that was going blind and he didn't have the heart to put him out of his misery, nor the money to keep feeding him.

He asked Ray to shoot his old faithful mule for him, and Ray said he would.

Now Brother Ray loves a good joke as much as anybody I know. On the way back to the truck, he got this great idea!

Pretending to be mad, Ray jumped into his truck and slammed the door. He said, "that ole rascal changed his mind and won't let us hunt on his place any more. I'm so mad. I'm gonna shoot one of his mules."

"You can't do that," his hunting buddy said. "Just watch me," said Ray. Then he grabbed his gun and went into the barnyard to put his neighbor's old blind mule out of his misery.

When he got back to the truck, he saw his friend had also taken his gun out and that smoke was a comin' from its barrel.

"What are you doing?" Ray shouted. His hunting buddy yelled back, "We'll show that son-of-a-gun. I'm so mad I just shot his cow!"

Of course, y'all know this mule story ain't exactly the whole truth, and that I told it for fun. It makes a good point though.

People usually do stupid things when they get angry — like shooting someone's cows. Try not to get too worked up, and I'll see you in church.
Brother Poor

Prayer by Mrs. Poor:

Forgive us, dear Lord, for saying and doing hateful and hurtful things. Amen.

KNEEL AND REJOICE

We sure did have ourselves a fine time in the big city of Raleigh this week. Why, there were preachers from all over gathered there — even the world editor of the Upper Room.

The lectures and sermons and singing were meaningful. But to me, the highlight of the seminar was when we stood in line and waited for space to kneel at the altar. Called men and women crowded around God's altar — confessing, reaffirming, and sincerely seeking God's guidance.

19

There we were, at the foot of the cross, kneeling — young and old, female and male, black and white and red and yellow, conservatives and liberals, high church and country, rich and poor, earned doctorates and high school dropouts, married and single, etc. — all sinners, saved by Grace, and called to preach the message:

"God created and loves the world — everyone and everything. God was in Christ, reconciling the world unto Himself. God has become incarnate — we are the visited planet. God will redeem the world — if we will repent of our sins and follow His will. God loves you — whoever you are!"

Brothers and sisters of the faith — worship in the church of your choice this weekend, and if your minister extends an altar call — kneel and rejoice. Even if you have to stand in line.   *Brother Poor*

Prayer by Mrs. Poor:

Dear Lord,

Whoever we are, wherever we are — enable us to know we are loved by You. Amen.

'SICK FOLK' EXPERIENCE
MIRACLE AFTER MIRACLE

Attendance at church last Sunday was mighty poor. Seems we had a goodly number of sick folk. So, after Sunday dinner, I figured I better get out and make a few visits. What I discovered made me rejoice! I saw miracle after miracle....

One of my favorite members, who had been deathly sick that very morning, had roused up and was riding down the road with his fishing pole. And then I saw brother Alton — his wife told me Sunday morning that her husband's back was in such foul shape that they were afraid an operation was gonna be necessary. Well, we remembered him in our prayers , and lo and behold, at 2 o'clock there he stood at the driving range hitting golf balls. Is that miraculous or what?

All told, about twenty of my sick folks had roused up and was taking nourishment in one form or another and enjoying the world. Mr. Webster, who don't attend church much 'cause he can't stand to be in crowds, was headed for the horse show. And sister Jane, bless her heart, who is too weak and too tired to get to church much, was out to the mall window shopping.

Oh, yes, Mike Barker's sister, who can't come out on account of her kidneys, stood in line about a hour to get into a two hour movie theater.

Yes sir, it thrilled my old heart to see what I saw. We oughta have a packed house next Sunday with all my sick folks healed and my shut-ins up and about. I just hope they don't overdo themselves before next Sunday and have a relapse.

Look forward to seeing you in church.
Brother Poor

Prayer by Mrs. Poor:

Help us to get our priorities straight, O Lord. Amen.

MAKE YOUR HEART A ROOM
WITH A VIEW

Do y'all remember the novel "A Room With a View"? In the book, Lucy Honeychurch is visiting in Italy with a friend. They're rich English people on another vacation, and when they get to a hotel, they want a room with a view.

What they mean is they want a room that looks out on the beautiful things of Italy — the marble statues, fine architecture, etc. However, there's only one room left, and it's on the wrong side of the hotel. It doesn't have a "view," at least not the kind of view they want. This room looks out over the marketplaces, viewing the poor people, the down-and-outers, the kind of people they don't want to know about. All the other rich people pity them. A room with no view! What a terrible way to spend the holidays!

The plot of the book: Lucy Honeychurch experiences conversion. Think of her name: "Honeychurch." Religion where everything is nice and pious and oh, so sweet! Then the author, E.M. Forster, changes her heart. He helps her to see the poor people. He has her reach out in compassion and touch their hurts and share their needs. She begins to see life as it really is for most of us. In the end, we get the feeling that Lucy Honeychurch actually does have "a room with a view."

If I might preach a bit: "Honey" is made by a bee who robs the beautiful flower of its nectar, and some of these flowers have briars on their stems. All sunshine makes a desert! Into every life some rain must fall. The good Lord does not spare even the best of us from pain. Suffering is universal! Sharing and sacrifice and service are what God's people do when they help to convert pain to gain, sorrows to brighter tomorrows, money into "milk and honey," and food and essentials for the poor.

Brother Poor

Prayer by Mrs. Poor:

Dear Lord,

Help us to convert pain to gain, sorrows to brighter tomorrows, and money to essentials for the poor. Amen.

NEW DREAMERS NEEDED

Martin Luther King, Jr., is dead (murdered) . . . but his dream still inspires . . . still offers hope . . . still lives . . . .

May his dream never be forgotten! May younger dreamers take up the nonviolent demonstrations and have the courage to walk the faith! May the spirit of Rev. King, may the spirit of the King of Kings, may the Holy Spirit, and the spirit of Christ sustain the dream and encourage new dreamers.

May we fulfill Martin's dream that one day "all of God's children, black and white, Jews and Gentiles, Protestants and Catholics [women and men], will be able to join hands and sing in the words of the old Negro spiritual, 'Free at last! Thank God almighty, we are free at last!' May we have the courage to put hands and feet to the dream. May Rev. Martin Luther King, Jr.'s, dream become our dream. And may all our dreams end in peace!

See you in church. *Brother Poor*

Prayer by Mrs. Poor:

Dear God,

Thanks for the dreams — and the dreamers. Amen.

DO UNTO OTHERS

We once owned a beautiful blue roan who could really do some fancy racking. It was our daughter's horse and she loved it dearly. It was some kind of sad though when we had to move to a new place with no room for our horse. I sold ole Blue to a man who we knew would take real good care of him.

To make a long story short — some years later, I was invited to preach a revival in a little North Carolina town down east. In the amen corner of the church sat the man I'd sold my horse to. Now, what if I'd a cheated him, or lied to him about Blue? That would have been a hard revival to preach, wouldn't it?

Of course, the moral of the story is to be honest in your horse trading, and treat the person you're doing business with just like you'd like to be treated. Do as our Christ taught: "Do unto others as you would have them do to you."

My paraphrase is — "Treat people fairly today, so you'll be able to look 'em in the eye tomorrow."

See you in church! *Brother Poor*

Prayer by Mrs. Poor:

Dear Lord,

May we not treat anyone badly in this old world. Amen.

27

HOLD ON TO WHATEVER ROPE
GOD PUTS IN YOUR HANDS

Me and Mrs. Poor just got back from St. Croix, down in the Virgin Islands. We flew out of Raleigh and stayed seven days down there. We was on a short-term volunteer-in-mission work team. We went in the name of our Christ and our church to work and to witness.

Mrs. Poor helped with the cooking, and there was no problem there. She can sure 'nuf bake big old country biscuits and stir up a real fine soup. She also helped paint a house for a widow lady and her two youngins.

Some of the team repaired a roof for a 83-year-old gentleman who lived alone. It was not a hard job for our carpenters, but was he ever so grateful. He asked God to bless us — we who came to help received the blessing!

Working with some more Christians from one of them Yankee states — I think it was Pennsavainie — we did a pretty big roof job on a parsonage. And then the real biggie — we painted a church roof that was high and steep.

My job was to help hold the rope that was thrown across the top of the church and then tied around the painter on the other side of the roof. His safety was literally in our hands. Reminded me of the time Paul's friends lowered him to safety over the Damascus wall. Remember? (Acts 9:25)

We had a most interesting time in St. Croix, but we sure was glad to be back home — where we have good drinking water and screens in our windows.

See you in church, brothers and sisters; and in the meantime, keep on holding on to whatever rope God may put into your hands.
Brother Poor

Prayer by Mrs. Poor:

Dear Lord,

Help us to keep holding on when times get difficult. Amen.

GOSPEL IS NOT ABOUT
SAVING OURSELVES

In one of his books, Norman Vincent Peale tells about a young man in North Carolina who was cruising timber in a swampy area. To make a long story short — the young fella soon found himself stuck in deadly quicksand, in the middle of the swamp, with no one around to help.

Nervously he unfastened his hip boots and dove for a root. Then slowly and carefully, inch by agonizing inch, he pulled himself out of his boots and then, out of the quicksand. He was safe! It had taken all of his strength — but he was safe.

Now it seems to me that this is a good story about how a lot of us think about our Christian faith. Someone asks, "Are you a Christian?" and we answer: "Well, I try to be" or "I'm trying to get myself together — or out of the depths of sin." But therein, brothers and sisters of the faith, we miss the joy of the Gospel. The Gospel is not about us pulling ourselves out of sin — but about a God of mercy and love who frees us with forgiveness and the gift of new life.   *Brother Poor*

Prayer by Mrs. Poor:

Dear Heavenly Father,

Thank you for the gift of eternal life through our Lord and Savior, Jesus Christ. Amen.

BACK TO THE BASICS IN BOTH FOOTBALL AND RELIGION

It's that time of year again when Mrs. Poor reads her Bible more, and prays more, and even does more preaching around the house. You see, it's football season now, and I usually go to a Friday night high school game, then watch a college game or two on Saturday T.V., then on Sunday evenings and Monday nights I watch the "pros."

Mrs. Poor claims she could take her clothes off and stand on her head by the television during a game and I'd never notice. But as far as I know, she ain't done it yet. But then again, maybe she has. Oh, well . . . .

31

Sometimes we men start talking football at the church before Sunday School. Someone mentions ole Vince Lombardi. Mr. Lombardi was often asked about trick plays and the secrets of coaching; he always answered that it was simply a matter of blocking and tackling. There were no new, clever ideas that really mattered unless one mastered the fundamentals of the game.

Now brothers and sisters of the faith, I've about concluded that the same is true in our spiritual life. Books, retreats, religious conferences are all the time promising us new "spirituality" — and some of them may stimulate us for a spell. But, in the end, we'll need to come back to "blocking and tackling" — such basic matters as studying the Sunday School lesson and praying and attending the church of your choice regularly. Whoops!! Gotta go now — they're giving out the scores on the late night news. See y'all in church, and at the games . . . . *Brother Poor*

Prayer by Mrs. Poor: *Dear Lord, May we study our Sunday School lessons and learn from your Holy Word daily. Amen.*

REASON FOR THE SEASON

A few years ago, I was pastoring a little church down on the beach near Wilmington. We decided we'd do one of them there live nativity scenes for Christmas. People volunteered to be shepherds, and wise men, and angels. We got a donkey and some sheep, picked Joseph and Mary; and some of the fellows who could carpenter built a manger — complete with straw and cows and chickens.

Then we got the idea of adding something to try to sorta bring tradition up to modern. We dared to do something different for Jesus . . . and most people got the message of Christmas in a new and more meaningful way.

At the very end of our nativity scene, after the shepherds had left their fields and bowed before the Christ child, and the three wise men had given their gifts, a fire truck pulled up with its siren sounding and Santa Claus got out!!!

Santa walked through the crowd carrying his big bag of toys, took off his hat and bowed down before the Christ child, with the shepherds on one side and the wise men on the other. *Brother Poor*

Prayer by Mrs. Poor:

"This Christmas O Lord, may we have a fresh insight into the true meaning of Christmas — the birthday of our Lord and Savior, Jesus Christ. And may we have the wisdom to explain to our children why Santa Claus should bow before Thy Son. Amen."

GANDHI OFFERED FOUR POINTS FOR SINCERE CHRISTIANS

Today's illustration comes from the movie "Gandhi." The Mahatma, which means "great soul," is fasting because of the fighting between the Hindus of India and the Muslims of Pakistan. It is a peace fast.

A Hindu soldier comes before Gandhi's bed and begs his forgiveness and asks for his prayers. He confesses he has killed a little Pakistani boy to avenge his own son's death. Mahatma Gandhi offers him (and us) this advice:

"Go," he says, "and adopt a Muslim youth and raise him as your own son — except for one difference — although you remain Hindu, train your adopted son to grow up to be a believer in the Muslim faith. Teach him the best of the Islamic religion; and expect the best from him. You will find that Hindu and Muslim can live together as one family."

When E. Stanley Jones, one of my favorite Methodist preachers, asked Gandhi, "The Great Soul," what he thought of "Christianity," he responded with four points:

"First, I would suggest that all of you Christians must begin to live more like Jesus Christ.

"Secondly, practice your religion without toning it down.

"Third, emphasize love and make it your working force, for love is central in Christianity.

"Fourth, study the non-Christian religions more sympathetically to find the good that is within them."

I believe "The Great Soul" was right.

1. We Christians worship Jesus more than we follow him.

2. Most of us would never think of rejecting Christ, we just reduce His gospel.

3. Jesus Christ was love personified, and we must follow His example.

4. Hindus and Muslims and Christians and Jews can live together as family — but in order to do this, we must respect each other and expect the best from each other.

See you folks at the church or synagogue or mosque of your choice.   *Brother Poor*

Prayer by Mrs. Poor:

Dear Lord, Help us to be more loving, especially to those with whom we differ. Amen.

PRAY FOR STRENGTH TO 'KICK' IN RIGHT DIRECTION

Ever heard the story 'bout the kicking mules who were maiming each other? Seems this herd of mules lived on a grassy plain near a forest. The grass was green and lush; the cool stream nearby made it an ideal spot, except it was near a forest where a large pack of hungry wolves lived.

Every evening, the wolves would come out of the forest in search of food. The mules would become frightened and begin kicking in every direction, maiming and injuring each other. Meanwhile, the wolves enjoyed a nice mule-burger for supper.

Finally, the mules wised up! The next time the wolves came, the mules put their heads together in a circle and began kicking outward. The wolves went without supper, and the mules did not harm each other.

Brothers and sisters of the faith, may the good Lord give you enough strength and wisdom to kick in the right direction at your next board meeting.
See you in church.   *Brother Poor*

Prayer by Mrs. Poor: *Dear Lord, Help us to see the wisdom of putting our heads together to solve problems. Amen.*

THERE AIN'T NO GOOD EXCUSE TO MISS CHURCH

We got to talking the other night after choir practice — or maybe I should say after quartet practice. We were wondering what we might do to improve church attendance some.

Sister Faith came up with the idea that we should have a "No-Excuse Sunday" — that way no one would have any excuse at all for not coming to church. Our new bass singer got us started out by saying he'd bring some steel helmets for those who say "the roof would cave in if they'd come to church!"

Ms. Hope said maybe we could put a putting green near the altar; and someone else suggested softer pews.

But it was Sister Charity, our alto singer (who's in the choir because of her looks, not because of her voice), who came up with probably the best idea. She said we should decorate the sanctuary with both Christmas poinsettias and Easter lilies for those who have never seen the church without them.

Well, excuses have always been around! So, if you've got a good one, hold on to it. 'Cause the times a comin' when ole St. Peter is gonna ask you for it. But let the truth be known, there ain't no good excuse! See you in church,   *Brother Poor*

Prayer by Mrs. Poor:

Dear Lord,

Please excuse us for making so many excuses. Amen.

DON'T SIT ON THE FENCE

I've always liked football. When we lived in Atlanta, I used to watch Georgia Tech 'bout every Saturday. But this one time, the Duke Blue Devils were playing Georgia Tech, and I didn't know what to do. You see, I'm a local boy from North Carolina, but I'd been following the Yellow Jackets all the while I was in Atlanta. Besides, this was back when Gene Berry was an all-American guard at Duke, and I had taught Gene in a Sunday school class when he was a boy.

Well, here's what happened. Whenever Tech would score, I'd applaud. And whenever Duke would move the ball, or Gene would break through and throw Tech for a loss, I'd shout my approval.

Finally, some guy behind me yelled: "Hey, buddy, make up your mind who you're for!"

Since then, I've thought lots about those words. For there are so many people in this old world who are rooting for both sides . . . fence sitters, we used to call them. They like the things of God, but they also like greed and indifference, etc. . . . To these people, I say this:

"Hey, buddy . . . Hey, sister . . . Hey, Mother and Dad . . . Make up your mind who you are for! If it is for Christ and His Church, then stand up. And if not, then get off the fence."

See you at the ball games, and in church.
Brother Poor

Prayer by Mrs. Poor: *Dear God,*
Help us to take a stand. Amen.

'HEY, CHURCH-GOERS'

Hope some of y'all like poetry. I call this poem "Hey, Church-Goers" . . . You are the only gospel that a lot of people will read . . . So as you ponder this poem, please take heed . . .

For it's not what we say,
     not even how "sincerely" we pray
It's more in how we live it, day by day . . .
     Not by "talking" it,
     But by "walking" it . . .

41

For the only gospel that a
   lot of people ever read
Is when they're sick or lonely,
   And we come to their need...
Or we ignore them, and they say
   "Huh! Christians indeed!"

For in a world of greedy, pleasure-
seeking, self-centered people . . .
The church is not judged by
   its landscape and lovely steeple.

Rather, the church is judged by...
   ... its love in action,
   ...its Christ-centered attraction.
   ...its commitment to mission,
   ...its "Great Commission".

There's another poem which I can't remember much of, but it goes something like this:

I'd rather see a sermon,
Than hear one any day . . .
I'd rather one walk with me,
Not just point out the way . .
   Brother Poor

Prayer by Mrs. Poor:

Dear Lord, Enable us to be walking sermons for those who don't take church seriously. Amen.

CAPTAIN NOAH GETS DRUNK

Since it has rained so much lately, I told a dear sister last Sunday I was thinking about building an ark. She reminded me of the rainbow and of God's promise to not do that again. Then I recalled an old mountain story I'd heard about Noah and the ark. It goes like this:

Seems some of Noah's neighbors used to laugh at him as he prepared for the flood. He became the laughing stock of the entire community. Then some teenagers, just for the fun of it, pulled a few nails from the bottom of the big boat. Their joke was on Noah, they thought. Sure 'nuf! The rains came — the rivers rose — the water covered the whole land. And only Captain Noah and his crew of twos rode out the storm.

43

But about 30 days into the severe weather — with cold rains descending, icy winds blowing down from the north, and glaciers floating by — the big boat sprung a leak!

As the story goes, the first to see the little nail hole leak was a monkey. He, of course, plugged the hole with his tail. He left his tail in the hole until it was about frozen off, and that's why, if you touch the tip of a monkey's tail today, you'll find it's still cold.

Well, the leak got bigger! And the next to come along was a dog. He stuck his nose in the hole to stop the leak for as long as he could. And that's why, when you touch the back of your hand to a dog's nose today, it's still cold.

Then along came Captain Noah. He sat down on the leak and sat there until the rains stopped and the ark landed. And that's why, when a man goes to warm himself by a fire today, he usually stands with his backside to the fire.

The above story of the ark leaking is not in the Bible; but this one is:

After Noah anchored, he built an altar and thanked God. Then he planted his crops and cultivated a vineyard, and then he got drunk.

If I was God, I'da probably lost all my patience then and there, and I'da drowned everybody — and made me some robots.

But sister's right! God has put a rainbow in the sky. He keeps his promise, though we often forget. He loves us, he forgives us, he lets us choose. We have freedom of choice. We can become sons and daughters of our Heavenly Father and endure the storms; or we can choose to go to that place where there ain't no water at all.

May we choose wisely.   *Brother Poor*

Prayer by Mrs. Poor:

God of Noah, God of Abraham, God of David, God of Isaiah, God of Peter, God of the pope, God of Martin Luther, God of the Wesleys, God of Billy Graham, God of the 21st Century, God of love, and mercy and justice, God of the universe, my God, our God. Amen.

UNCOMMON ANSWER TO A COMMON QUESTION

In answer to the question "How are you doing?" some of us say, "Well, I'm still in one piece." Last Sunday I preached on that phrase, but I put a different slant on it. The sermon was entitled "Still, in One, Peace." It's a three-pointer and the outline looks like this:

1. "STILL" — "Be still and know that I am God" — Psalm 46:10. Jesus spent lots of time in meditation, and so must we. Everybody needs a Garden of Gethsemane if we are going to follow God's will and way.

2. "IN ONE" — Paul writes in Ephesians 4: "There is one body, and one Spirit, even as ye are called in one hope of your calling: One Lord, one faith, one baptism. One God and Father of all . . . "

The important question is not whether we are Southern Baptists or Free Will Baptists or Independent Baptists — the question is, are we Christian Baptists? For if we sincerely call God

Father, then we as brothers and sisters of the faith are "in one."

3. "PEACE" — When I got to this point in the sermon, I asked one of our fine young singers to let the Holy Spirit bless us with his notes. He sang these words: "Let there be peace on earth; and let it begin with me."

Hope to see you in church; but in the meantime, May you remain "Still, in One, Peace."

Brother Poor

Prayer by Mrs. Poor:

Dear God,

Help me to be still, to worship you, and to know thy Peace. Amen.

BIBLES ARE MEANT TO BE READ, NOT FORGOTTEN

What if our family Bible kept a diary? It might read something like this:

Jan. 1 —   My owner made a New Year's resolution that he was going to read from me every day of the year.

Jan. 2-10 — My owner did read from me every day — at first quite a bit, but then less and less.

Jan. 11 — Back on the table again, collecting dust.

Feb. 3 — I was picked up, dusted off, and placed back on the table.

April 5 — A lock of the baby's hair was placed within my cover.

April 12 — A recipe and two snapshots were added.

May 8 — Again, dusted off and placed back on the table.

The week of July 4th, we went on vacation. I think we went to the beach because it was hot and stuffy in the suitcase where I stayed. Really, they could have left me home . . . .

July 11 — Taken out of the suitcase and placed back on the table.

Aug. 7 — Grandmother came to visit. She read from me often — and occasionally a tear would fall on my pages.

Aug. 14 — Grandmother left, but before she did, she held me gently in her lap for a long time.

Oct. 5 — I was picked up, dusted off, and placed back on the table.

Nov. 12 — Mr. Brown, the head of the household, used me to find some references for a Sunday School class. He had a pretty hard time finding them, although they were in the same place all the time.

Dec. 10 — Little Johnny read from the gospel of Luke. He was trying to memorize the scripture about the shepherds. I think maybe it should read like this: "And there were in the same country, hypocrites, abiding in the land, keeping watch over their Bibles . . . and reading them . . . not!"

Still, in One, Peace. *Brother Poor*

Prayer by Mrs. Poor: *Dear God, speak to us through the Bible, and then speak through us to the world. Amen.*

Saved to Serve

It was 94 degrees on the outside, but I was laid back in my big, soft desk chair — feet propped up — cooling it in my nice air-conditioned office. I had just prayed, asking God to give me an idea or two to get my next Sunday's sermon started. I was thumbing through some church magazines when somebody knocked at my door.

"Who in the world would be bothering me at this time of the morning," I thought. I opened the door to a middle-aged man who looked sort of down and out; yet he had a certain look of authority about him. He said, "Preacher, I need some help."

"Well, come on in," I said. "You can cool off a bit and discuss your problem with me, and we'll try to make things right."

"But my needs are out here," he said, "In my house, on the farm where I work, in the school where my children study. You come out here." I told the stranger I was working on my sermon, but I could spare him some time if he'd come on in.

He insisted I ride with him over to his house. As we drove down the street, he asked me if I knew who lived in certain houses he'd point out.

I'd tell him the names of the people, and he'd tell me things about them.

"Listen," I said, starting to feel sorta rotten. "They know where the church is, and they know when we meet. They're welcome to come join us in singing and praying, and hearing the preaching."

As he brought me back to the church office and let me out, the stranger's last words to me were: "Preacher, if you want the people to listen to you on Sunday, then you ought to visit them during the week and listen to them."

'Course the above story didn't actually happen. I just dozed off a little, sitting there in my comfortable chair and nice office, and dreamed of that knock on my door. But the point is still well made.

We need to get people to church. But the other side of the coin — we need to get the church to the people. Jesus did both, and those of us who are Christ-like and who realize we have been saved to serve, must do both also. See you in church; and let's make sure that the people see the church in us.   *Brother Poor*

Prayer by Mrs. Poor: *Dear Lord, may people see the church in me. Amen.*

BELIEVERS IN JESUS NEED NOT FEAR DEATH

It's about time for the radio stations to start playing one of my favorite Christmas songs, "Grandma Got Run Over by a Reindeer"! I guess I like it 'cause I sorta identify with grandpa. I like that line: "As for me and grandpa, we believe."

Well, the other night, it happened to me. I was driving through Flowers Swamp; it was foggy and dark. This big, old buck jumped out of nowhere and just stood there defiantly, right in the middle of my half of the road. I tried to miss him, but it happened so quickly. In fact, it took me a minute or so to realize what had happened.

By then, the deer had gone back into the swamp. I don't know how bad he got hurt (if any), but he sure tore up the front end of my car.

After it was all over, I got out to examine the damage. I tried to stop two passing cars for help, but there was no way anyone with good sense was going to stop in that dark swamp. (One of my headlights was smashed out.) I felt sorta like the victim on the Jericho Road before the Good Samaritan arrived.

But then, the passers-by didn't know I was Brother Poor — I could have been brother I. B. Mean or brother I. R. Bad. I hate to admit it, and I know it goes against Scripture, but I'd probably a passed on by myself; and I certainly would have wanted my wife to.

The bottom line to this experience: That deer could have been jumping and could have come over the hood of my car and come through the window and killed me dead. Rev. I. R. Poor could have instantly become Rev. I. M. Dead. Reminds me of the sobering thought: "Life is short; death is sure. Sin is the wound; Christ is the cure."

Are you cured? Go to the church of your choice this weekend, and join me and Grandpa as believers. In the meantime, watch out for them deers. *Brother Poor*

Prayer by Mrs. Poor:

Dear Lord, Thank you for Jesus Christ and the assurance of life after death. Amen.

FORGIVEN' AN' FORGETTIN'

I know a couple who went to a funeral a while back, and they wuz the onliest ones who showed up — no other people, no casket, no preacher. After a while of sitting in that empty church, they figured it out — they wuz either at the wrong church or had the wrong time.

The husband had just glanced at the paper, but he felt sure he had the right time. So they drove from Broad Ridge over to Long Branch — and sho' 'nuff, there wuz the funeral — complete with hearse and everything.

Reminded me of a time when I wuz a preachin' over in the Greenville area. They called me from a neighboring church and said that they wuz all there — the bride, the groom, the people — but no preacher. They asked if I'd come over and help 'em out. Well, I wuz a mowin' the grass, so I jes' put on my robe and went right on over.

The piano player, who was the assistant ECU football coach's wife, and a good friend, told me later she was never more glad to see a preacher. She had been playing for a long, long time. And besides, it was some kinda' hot in that little chapel.

Seems the preacher had gotten his schedule confused and he had taken his family to the beach. Oh, well, we all make mistakes. Just as long as we get to our own funeral on time. Besides, I'm sorta countin' on the good Lord havin' a sense of humor. And I know personally, He understands and forgives mistakes.   *Brother Poor*

Prayer by Mrs. Poor:

Dear Lord, Let me learn from my mistakes.

KEEP ROMANCE IN MARRIAGE

One of my favorite stories is one Randy Travis told at the state fair a few years back. Mr. Travis was then a very popular country sanger.

It's 'bout a couple who sat down front at one of Randy's shows 'cause the wife couldn't hear too good. The husband repeated things for her by yelling in her ear.

Well, in between songs, Randy told us he grew up in Marshville, N.C. The wife asked her husband, "What'd he say?" The husband yelled in her ear, "He says he's a North Carolina boy."

Mr. Travis next told the audience he now lived in Tennessee near the Grand Ole Opry House. Again the wife asked, "What'd he say? The husband yelled, "He now lives in Nashville."

Then Randy told us about the last time he had come to Raleigh. He was single then and someone fixed him up with a blind date. He said it was a real bad night — the girl was not only fat and ugly, she also had a retarded personality. 'Bout that time the man's wife asked, "What'd he say?" The husband leaned over and yelled in her ear, "He says he thinks he might know you!"

That story sorta reminds me of the old adage:

> Beauty is skin deep —
> Ugly is to the bone.
> Beauty fades away;
> Ugly holds its own.

But let me add a line or two, okay?

> She may be fat, ugly and slow —
> But if she's a good Christian woman,
> Don't be foolish enough To let her go.
> For beauty is not only skin deep,
> beauty is also in the eye of the beholder.
> Let me tell you young folk something
> true love gets better as you get older!

Keep that romance going,   *Brother Poor*

Prayer by Mrs. Poor:

Dear Lord, help me and Brother Poor to keep on loving each other. Amen.

GOD IS BLIND TO THE UGLINESS OF OUR SIN

I just wrote y'all a story about Randy Travis dating an ugly North Carolina girl. To sorta get the women off my case, I'm gonna write about an ugly man — I mean sure 'nuf ugly.

Now mind you, he wasn't poor. In fact, he was a very wealthy young man. His parents had left him very well off. He had all that a person could want — materially. But he had been born with a deformity which left him with a very ugly face.

Because of his ugliness, he stayed home all the time and worked a lot in his garden which was closed in by a high wall. Sometimes at night, he would walk down by the seashore. One such night, he heard some real pretty music. He hid himself in the shadows, and there he saw a young woman playing the violin.

Thereafter, each night he would leave his house, walk down to the seashore and listen to the young lady play her beautiful music. But because of his ugliness, he continued to hide in the shadows.

By telephone and certified letter, this young-ugly-wealthy "in love" man worked out a deal whereby the girl could go to the best school of music in Europe. After years of study, she returned home and, at her request, was taken to the house of the man who had paid for her education.

He was standing in the garden, with his back to her. The gate was opened for her, and she came up behind him, threw her arms around him and cried out, "I love you — I love you!"

"Oh, no," he exclaimed, "that's impossible!" Turning around, he said, "How could you ever love someone as ugly as me?" "Oh, my generous darling," she replied. "I thought you knew — I'm blind."   *Brother Poor*

Prayer by Mrs. Poor: *In the sense that true love is blind to ugliness, we thank thee, Lord. Amen.*

IF YOU WANT TO MAKE 'EM HAPPY, DON'T TEACH, PREACH OR UMPIRE

Now I knowed that just as soon as I started writin' this here story 'bout the Lord, I'd step on somebody's toes. Anytime you say you are for something — two or three people will speak up against it.

Back when I was a young fella, I used to umpire some high school games. I felt that was a purty good thing for a preacher to do — I really didn't care who won, I just wanted to help them abide by the rules, and play fair, and let the best team win. Besides, I thought the fans would know that a preacher wouldn't cheat . . . .

Ha! Boy, was I wrong! I got called some words we sure don't teach in Sunday School. If you folks ever gonna call some "balls and strikes" — you better put some cotton in your ears.

60

Listen, whenever a game's tied and a player rounds third and heads home and the throw from right field gets there at the same time — or purty near the same time — and everybody on the field and in the stands looks at you for the call . . . .

At a time like that — and you can expect them to come up every now and then — either way you call it, you're going to make some people real happy and some people real unhappy.

If you are the kind of person who is trying to satisfy everybody all the time — then forget umpiring, and preaching, and taking a stand on any decision-making issue.

The old paraphrase is right: "You can satisfy all the people some of the time, and even some of the people all the time — but no one can satisfy all the people all of the time." Not even our blessed "crucified" Lord! See y'all in church! *Brother Poor*

Prayer by Mrs. Poor: *Help us to have the courage to "call 'em as we see 'em," O Lord. No — enable us to "call them as Jesus sees them." Amen.*

Spring Cleaning

Now that summer is almost gone, me and the Mrs. have got around to doing our spring cleaning. She decided we'd move the book-cases around. I'd forgotten how many books I had! When we were about through, Mrs. Poor said, "I. R., if you knew half of what's in these books, you'd be twice as smart as you are now."

Of all my books, my favorites are ones that have been written by friends. There's something kinda special about knowing the author. But then, of all my books, the Holy Bible is by far my favorite. Why?

Because I know the Author, and He has written some things in it specially for me. God knows your name also, my friend, and He's got a message or two in His word for you.

The Bible is a Holy Book about men who were searching for God. But it is also about a God who is searching for men. Read it — it's a great way to get right with God and to learn how to get right with your fellow men and women.

Well, I gotta get back to work now. Mrs. Poor has decided to move everything back just like it was when we first started.   *Brother Poor*

Prayer by Mrs. Poor: *Dear Loving Father, Help us to put hands and feet to our Bible reading. Amen.*

WEDDING AT CANA MAKES
FOR A 3-POINT SERMON

We sure are having ourselves a bunch of weddings out in our neck of the woods. So to sorta "go with the flow," I preached about Jesus attending a marriage in Cana. It's a three-point sermon. Sometimes I just preach one-point theme sermons, and Mrs. Poor declares that ever now and then I preach some "no-point" sermons. Oh, well! I call this here sermon: "How Jesus Turned Water Into Wine." You need to pick up your Bible and read John 2:1-11, or you really won't understand the rest of this story.

Point No. 1: Mary, the mother of Jesus, took her problem to Jesus. We should do the same thing.

Point No. 2: Mary's advice is, "Do whatever Jesus says!" And that ain't bad advice either. When you hear the voice, and you get the feeling, do like the t-shirt reads: "Just do it."

Point No. 3: How did Jesus work this miracle? He worked through the hands and minds of the servants. How does Jesus work miracles today? — through his servants . . .   *Brother Poor*

Prayer by Mrs. Poor:

May Jesus' presence be felt in all Christian marriages. Amen.

Take Time To Help
A Friend in Need

My good friend, Chaplain Corbin Cherry, lives way out in California. He crosses the Golden Gate bridge twice about every day on his way to and from work. Coming home one evening, he saw a woman climb up on the rail and start to jump off into the bay (suicide).

He stopped his car in the middle of traffic and called out to the lady and tried to give her some reasons to live. And what's even better, when she began to talk, he listened!

I'm pleased to tell you she decided to give us Christians another chance to help her find the abundant life. But I'm disgusted to tell you that while my friend was witnessing to her, people in their cars began to blow their car horns and yelled, "Either jump or get back in the car. We're in a hurry, and you're blocking our way."

Can you believe it? CAN YOU BELIEVE IT? People in too big a hurry to stop and help and try to save someone. Wonder where they were in such a big hurry to get to?   *Brother Poor*

Prayer by Mrs. Poor:

Open our eyes, Lord, that we may see opportunities to help. Amen.

Moms, Dads Seen as 'Light of the World'

Well, another Vacations Bible School has done come and gone. Children from all over the community came out for the fun and games and music and study . . . and the hurt feelings and the pushing and the tears and the silence that sometimes comes when a little girl is supposed to sing a solo or a little boy recites a verse of scripture.

Reminds me of the time a little fellow had to stand before the congregation and simply say: "I am the Light of the World."

However, like many of us in this old world, when he stood up, his memory sat down. He just stood there — unable to speak. Then his mother leaned out into the aisle and whispered: "I am the Light of the World."

Whereupon, Little Johnny rared back and said loud and clear: "My Mother is the Light of the World."

Moms, dads, you are the light of the world to your children until they are old enough to decide for themselves. Don't wait until next year to bring your child back to church. Take your child to the church of your choice this Sunday; and may the light and love of Jesus reflect in your life and in your parental guidance.   *Brother Poor*

Prayer by Mrs. Poor:

Dear Lord,

As concerned parents in this darkening world, may we help our children discover the "Light of the World," Jesus Christ. Amen.

MAN OVERCOMES TRAGEDY TO BRIGHTEN OTHERS' LIVES

We had a one-legged man preach in our pulpit last week, and man could he preach and sing. He is an old friend of mine since school days. We've done lots of things together, and we love and respect each other very much. He walks what he talks, and that to me makes his preaching worth listening to. Jesus said, "follow me," and his preachers ought to be able to say the same. "Do as I say and not as I do" don't get it for me.

My friend lost his leg when he stepped on a mine in Vietnam. He went flying one way and his leg went another.

Now that's worth crying about — and complaining — and becoming bitter and/or feeling sorry for yourself. But not my friend! Instead of fussing, he learned to pick a guitar and started making up happy tunes to brighten the life of others. He set up wheelchair races in the hospital. He learned to play golf on one leg. He softened up the hard cases with his jokes and winning personality. He became a wounded healer. He preached of God's love every chance he got; and when he got out of the hospital, he became a V.A. chaplain.

I asked him his secret. "Every morning, I put my best foot forward," he laughed. "And I ask the Good Lord to help me walk in His footprint. Daily, I try to impress on others that God loves them; and because of Christ, so do I."

If my friend can do all this on one leg, seems to me those of us with two legs ought to be doing a little bit more for our Lord.

See you in church. *Brother Poor*

Prayer by Mrs. Poor:

Dear Lord,

As Brother Poor's friend witnesses on one leg, may we be inspired to do more on our two. Amen.

ROAST SKUNK

A woman lived next door to a private zoo. She called up the police and told them she had a skunk in her cellar. "Open the cellar door," the officer suggested. "Make a trail of bread crumbs from the cellar to the garden. Then wait for the skunk to follow it outside."

Half an hour later the woman called a second time. "I did what you said . . . now I got two skunks in my cellar."

Question: "How can we get the "stink" out of our lives?"

Answer: "Just accept the good Lord's forgiveness, and follow Jesus."

Speaking of skunks . . . A preacher was invited home with a family to eat Sunday dinner with them. While the mom and dad were in the kitchen putting the final touches on the meal, the preacher asked the little daughter what they were having today." The little girl said, "Skunk."

"Skunk?" said the preacher. "You know not."

"That's right," said the little girl. "When Mama told Daddy you were coming for dinner today, Daddy said, "You mean we're having that old skunk again today?"

Needless to say, Mama's roast tasted a little peculiar that Sunday.

See you in church, and maybe for Sunday dinner someday.   *Brother Poor*

Prayer by Mrs. Poor:

Remind us, O Lord, that we shouldn't say anything that we do not want our children to hear and/or repeat. Amen.

"Honk, If You Love Jesus"

I enjoy reading t-shirts and bumper stickers, don't y'all? I 'specially like the one that reads: **"Support Mental Heath Or I'll Kill You."** It sorta gets your attention, you know what I mean?

And how 'bout the one written in very small print: ". . . if you can read this, you are too close!" It's not hard to get the message that we shouldn't tail gate, and that we should drive unto others as we would like for others to drive unto us.

But let me tell you a story about a bumper sticker. Seems my Presbyterian preacher friend saw this bumper sticker that read: "Honk, If You Love Jesus!" Well, my friend is a pretty educated fella; and for some reason, the thought just didn't sit right with him. He first thought it was pretty trite, then the more he thought about it, the more he thought there might be something to it. After all, why not communicate with a fellow Christian? It might brighten his day and encourage him to make a better witness. Finally, he decided he'd do it. Just before the light turned green, he honked his horn — and guess what happened?

The fellow got out of his car, walked back to my friend's car, and said, "Listen, you blankity-blank impatient moron, that light hadn't even turned to green when you blew your blame horn. Why didn't you start sooner if you are in such a hurry!" Then he got back in his car, slammed his door, and took off . . . leaving my friend sitting at the red light with a red face . . . embarrassed for the "Christian" who was wearing his religion on the bumper of his car.

It seems to this old sinner that it don't much matter about the label on the outside . . . whether you are a Presbyterian, or a Baptist, or a Untied Methodist. It's whether you drive unto others as you would have others drive unto you that counts.
Brother Poor

Prayer by Mrs. Poor:

Dear Lord, may we be careful as we drive to the church of our choice this Sunday. Amen.

WHAT IF?

It's homecoming time! Me and Mrs. Poor and the kids are sure bud enjoying visiting with some of you folks we haven't seen in a while. Ain't it nice to eat fried chicken and hear some good preaching and singing and eat fried chicken and visit with old friends and eat some more fried chicken? Mrs. Poor told me Sunday that if I ate one more chicken wing, there'd be no need to get in the car — I could just fly home!

And what better text to preach on homecoming Sunday than the prodigal son, Luke 15. I called my sermon "What If?"

What if the father had not given his youngest the money and let him go? Y'all reckon he'd ever have "come to his senses"?

What if the father had welcomed his repentant son back with these words: "See there, boy, I told you so. If you had only listened to me in the first place."

What if the mother had said, "Well, it's about

74

time you came back. Do you know the heartbreak you've caused me — the sleep I've lost over you — the way you've made your daddy worry while you were away?"

What if the elder brother had rushed in from the field and hugged him and shouted, "Thank God, you've seen the light! Welcome home, my brother, I sure have missed you. It's great to have you home." Talk about a homecoming! And one more what if . . .

What if a newcomer comes to your church this Sunday and no one welcomes him or her, and no one gets their name, and no one telephones them on Monday, and no one takes them a pie, and no one says to them, "Welcome!"
What if . . . .   *Brother Poor*

Prayer by Mrs. Poor:

Dear God,

What if You really did forgive us our sins as we forgive those who have offended us. Amen.

GOD'S CHECKLIST

My brother died recently of cancer of the throat. When I went to the hospital during his last hours, he asked me to do his eulogy. I told him I didn't think I could do that; but he insisted, so I tried. I had officiated at his wedding, and now at his funeral . . . but his eulogy was the hardest thing I've had to do in my 35-year ministry.

Before he died, he said to me, "Brother, if you were going to jump out of an airplane, I could teach you how and give you a checklist." (My brother was an ex-paratrooper, and an all-the-way airborner.) He continued, aided by his voice box: "I've got to make that last jump soon, and you can teach me how. Let's go over that checklist. I just want to make sure I'm truly saved."

Now folks, you can believe I touched all the basics as I explained God's plan of salvation to my little brother, six years my junior. I recalled how, when we were little boys, how daddy used to give us a big Christmas with lots of nice things. Not because we deserved it, but just because he loved us. In like manner, God's gift of salvation is ours, not because we deserve it, but because God loves us. Ours is to repent of our sins and accept the gift.

Finally, I reminded him of how, when we were kids, sometimes when we would be watching late-night T.V., that he would go to sleep in the den and dad would carry him off to the bedroom. Next morning, he would wake up in his bed, not knowing how he got there. I told Ralph that death was just like that. That we simply go to sleep here, trusting God's grace, and wake up there. Somehow, someway, Someone carries us to another "house with many mansions in it," and we wake up there.

A few hours later, he went to sleep and made that final jump! Whoever you are, sooner or later, you too are gonna wake up dead. Are you ready?

See you in church.   *Brother Poor*

Prayer by Mrs. Poor: *Dear Lord, like the Boy Scout motto, may we "be prepared." Amen.*

GOOD NEWS/BAD NEWS

I wish to introduce this story with a very bad joke; however, it sets up the plot very well. So, here goes:

The physician tells his patient, "I have some good news and some bad news for you. The good news is: the results of your examination reveals that you have only three days to live."

"That's the good news?" shouts the patient. "What in the world is the bad news?"

Doctor: "The bad news is that I have been trying to get up with you for the last two days." (See, I told you it was a bad joke.)

Now, I've got some good news and some bad news for y'all! The bad news is that in this old world, there is sin, disease, old age, and death. The good news is that our spirits, our souls, will live forever; and that God, via the Holy Spirit, suffers with us during these difficult times.

The bad news is that there are many people like Judas still around today — who will do almost anything to get hold of someone else's money. The good news is that there are a lot of committed "stewards" who, like Zacchaeus, have had salvation come to their home. (Luke 19:1-10)

The bad news is there are diseases like cancer, diabetes, sickle cell . . . . The good news is that God is working through the skilled hands and trained minds of the men and women in our hospitals and cancer institutes.

The bad news is that life has suffering and pain and funerals. The good news is that "Jesus wept" — that Jesus suffered a painful death on a cross — that Jesus understands suffering and pain and funerals — that "Jesus Saves!"

The bad news is that there are still people who are "lost" and have not experienced the saving power of God Almighty. The "Good News" is that salvation is possible — via repentance, acceptance and dedication.   *Brother Poor*

Prayer by Mrs. Poor: *Thank You, dear God, for changing the bad news of the crucifixion into the Good News of the resurrection. Amen.*

KEEP ON KEEPING ON

We got on the elevator together, and we were the onliest passengers. He wore a black shirt with a white collar and carried a Bible. So I said to him in sort of a break-the-ice tone, "Sir, you've got your shirt on back-wards." Really, I'd wanted to say that 'bout all my life anyhow.

He laughed warmly, like he'd heard that one before. Gave me the opportunity to introduce myself and to inquire as to his denomination. He was serving a Lutheran church in the big city of Charlotte, N.C.

I had just read in the newspaper and knew of his church's bad publicity about "sexuality." "You folks have given the news media a field day," I commented. "Let's see . . . okaying homosexual marriages, and pre- or non-marital affairs."

He was quick to point out that the newspaper had printed only parts of the report of a sub-committee, that they had taken that out of context, and that the report was not speaking for the

Lutheran church, but was a statement to be presented to the church for discussion and vote.

I told him I knew the feeling. A few years back, our denomination had put together a new hymnal. Some of our liberals felt the "Battle Hymn of the Republic" was too militant. Our conservatives, who probably didn't even look at the words, liked the tune and the fact that the hymn was good enough for their grandparents (tradition). The newspapers sure played that up.

Well, I was just getting warmed up about the time that elevator put us off. As we walked to our separate cars, I put my arm around my new-young-Lutheran-preacher-priest-pastor-buddy and said: "Keep on keeping on . . . even when they don't want to hear that Jesus loves us all. Tell 'em anyway, and then show 'em by your lifestyle. You may have your shirt on backwards, but you'll always have your head on straight." *Brother Poor*

Prayer by Mrs. Poor: *Dear Lord, May more preachers of different denominations meet up in more elevators. May they share their 'ups and downs.' Amen.*

TOLSTOY'S PARABLE

One of the immortal parables of Jesus is his parable of the man who wanted to build bigger barns, and then fill them with more and more. He had as much as he needed, but that did not satisfy him. He wanted to lay up so much more so that he could take his ease, eat, drink, and be merry the rest of his days. In short, he was so wrapped up in himself he had no concern for others. (Luke 12:13)

There is a Russian legend which is in tune with Jesus' parable — the legend of a peasant who could never be content because he was always hearing of richer lands that could be had in the next province beyond his own. In Tolstoy's parable, the man will be given all the land he can walk around in a day.

Early the next morning, he started out ... his eyes shining with delight at this fertile soil that was to soon be his. Noon came, and still he went straight on. The land was too good for him to turn to alter his course, so that he might bend the boundary and enclose the area which would soon be his.

The afternoon passed, and the shadows began to lengthen. He was a long way from his starting point. On he went with desperate haste, his muscles aching, the blood beating in his ears. A long way off, he saw the starting point as the sun went down, with a crowd of people watching to see whether he would make it.

He drove himself with one final terrific effort, swayed forward to claim his new possessions, staggered, and fell down dead . . . .

Jesus asked, "What does it profit a man if he gain the whole world and lose his soul?" Amen.
Brother Poor

Prayer by Mrs. Poor:

Teach us to share, Lord; teach us to share. Amen.

Ben Franklin

Old Ben Franklin did more than fly a kite in the rain and invent bifocal spectacles. "Poor Richard's Almanac" influenced the life of many; and he was one of the five men who drafted the "Declaration of Independence." He also had some deep thoughts on religion. But first, lets consider some of his Almanac statements:

Fish and visitors stink after three days!

Content makes poor men rich.
Discontent makes rich men poor.

Little strokes fell great oaks.

You will be careful if you are wise
how you touch men's religion, credit and eyes.

Franklin's rendition of the Lord's prayer is as follows: "Heavenly Father, may all revere Thee, and become Thy dutiful children and faithful subjects. Provide for us this day as Thou has hitherto daily done. Forgive us our trespasses, and enable us to forgive those who offend us. Keep us out of temptation, and deliver us from evil. Amen."

A few weeks before he died, Benjamin Franklin wrote to Ezra Stiles, then president of Yale University: "Here is my creed . . . I believe in one God, Creator of the Universe. That He governs it by His Providence. That He ought to be worshiped. That the most acceptable service we render Him is doing good to His other children. That the soul of man is immortal, and will be treated with justice in another life respecting its conduct in this. These I take to be the principles of sound religion, and I regard them in whatever sect I meet with them."

"As to Jesus of Nazareth, I think His system of morals and His religion, as He left them to us, the best the world ever saw or is likely to see; but I apprehend it has received various corrupt changes. I have some doubts as to His divinity; though it is a question I do not dogmatize upon, and think it needless to busy myself with it now, when I expect soon an opportunity to know the truth with less trouble."

Benjamin Franklin died on April 17, 1790, at the age of eighty-four . . . and as he prophesied, he now knows the truth about Jesus Christ. Do you? Amen.   *Brother Poor*

Prayer by Mrs. Poor:

Remind us, O Lord, that Jews, Muslims and Christians all trace their origin through Abraham to You; and while we may pray to You using different words and different rituals, we each recognize You as our Creator - God. Amen.

PASTOR HILL

I have a black preacher friend who used to be an alcoholic. He saw the light, and is now trying to help others out of the darkness. Now Pastor Hill don't know much about systematic theology or sociology or clinical psychology; but he knows a good deal about the Lord and about conversion.

Where whiskey bottles used to sit on the shelf, bread and milk for the babies sit now. Where he used to fight with his wife, he sits now and reads the Bible to his family. And where he used to fall drunken in self-pity, he now kneels and thanks God for life.

The other day, I asked him, "Pastor Hill, you ever think about drinking again?"

And he says, "No sir, I was a fool to ever start messing with that stuff. I used to say I could drink a little and loosen up and then things would get better. Well, the truth of the matter was . . . I didn't drink just a little, I drank a whole lot. And things didn't get better, they got worser! I ne'r 'bout died. They sent me to Cherry Hospital to dry me out, and I had my first sober thoughts in years. It was there that the Lord called me. He forgave me my wicked ways and gave me another life. And I'll tell you something, Rev. Poor, I ain't never had it so good. And I love to preach about God's power to save and change lives!"

Friends, I too love to preach about God's power to save. How 'bout you? Have you seen the light? Put on your Sunday clothes and go do church this Sunday. God's power will be waiting for you. Amen.

Brother Poor

Prayer by Mrs. Poor:

Do it again, Lord; do it again and again until our land is free of alcohol addicts. Amen.

SANTA GOD

It seems to me that the problem with most of us is that we have a concept of a Santa Claus-God. We feel that if we are good and go to church, our Santa God will bless us and give us good things.

And in a like manner, if we are mean and sinful, ole Jesus Claus will put switches in our stockings or cause us to suffer. This is a very childish concept of a God of love, to say the least.

God is not a Santa Claus with a long white beard, sitting up in the sky recording good and bad marks in a book of judgment, with a goodlooking son sitting at his right hand. This is only a god created in man's image and given the powers of a superman.

The God of the Holy Bible is a Person, but not contained in a physical body as we are. God is Spirit. In fact, God is the true Spirit of Christmas. Do you have the **Christ**-mas Spirit? *Brother Poor*

Prayer by Mrs. Poor: *Fill us with thy Christmas Spirit, O Lord. Amen.*

Happiness Is ...

I'm in a serious mood today, so let me share with you my answer to the question: "What is happiness?"

Happiness is being loved; and finding someone in this world with whom you can share love. "And God said, 'It is not good that man should be alone.' And he gave man a help mate." (Genesis 2:18)

Happiness is baby diapers, rocking your dreams in your arms in the wee hours of the morning, and burps. Happiness is responsibility and sacrifices for loved ones. Happiness is healing a scratched knee with a band-aid and a kiss.

Happiness is listening to young minds, and catching glimpses of their dreams, and rapping with teenagers about values. Happiness is giving away your daughter's hand in marriage or gaining another son. Happiness is becoming a grandparent and maturing and adjusting to the fact of death and the hope of eternity.

Happiness is freedom to choose . . . That is, to choose one's goals, one's gods, one's good.

Happiness is learning together today for a better tomorrow, having wholesome feelings about the past, and living excitingly and meaningfully in whatever present we know.

Happiness is Christianity — "A way of life based on love and truth and beauty as these elements culminate in the teachings of Christ."

Happiness is being a part of God's creative love.

Brother Poor

Prayer by Mrs. Poor:

Help us, Lord God, to better understand the third chapter of Proverbs and Jesus' Beatitudes. For that, to me, is what happiness is. Amen.

SHARING THE PEACE

It seems to me that the first business of the church is not to turn the world upside down, but to turn human hearts right side up. Our ultimate objective undoubtedly is a new heaven and a new earth, but it begins with new hearts and heavenly conduct. We might rightfully hope to transform the world but only through redeemed men and women.

You say, "but what can I, one person, do?" Let me cite this illustration: An official of a great industrial organization in Chicago was in consultation with an associate from another city. The subject of the church entered the conversation. "I had an extremely interesting experience last night," the Chicago man said. "Two men came to my house to talk with me about becoming a Christian and joining the church. It made quite an impression on me that they should come to my home on a rainy night to talk the matter over with me."

The other said, "That is strange . . . for last week a couple of visitors were over at my house, too, on the same errand. That's quite a coincidence!"

While they were discussing the matter, an executive from the East came in and heard some comment about the church. "Men," he said, "what you are saying about the church reminds me of a very significant thing that happened to me a little more than a week ago. A couple of laymen appeared at my home one evening to talk to me about becoming a Christian and uniting with the church."

The three looked at each other in frank surprise. Three men from Chicago, Atlanta, and New York had been visited within a week in the name of Christ and the church. And that kind of persistent evangelism, my friends, has unlimited possibilities.

What can you do? Look around you, listen, and share! *Brother Poor*

Prayer by Mrs. Poor:

Show us the wisdom of lay visitation, O, Lord. If each one could reach one in the name of Christ, our church would double in membership. Amen..

ELVIS PRESLEY

Six weeks before he died, Elvis Presley was asked by a reporter, "Elvis, when you started playing music, you said you wanted three things in life: You wanted to be rich, you wanted to be famous, and you wanted to be happy. Are you happy, Elvis?"

"No," Elvis replied. "I'm lonely as hell."

Rich, famous, but lonely. At first, Elvis' remark seemed offensive to me. But then, the more I thought about it, I guess he was right. Elvis' comment is well put. I suppose Hell is a lonely place.

A Chicago woman died after jumping off the 14th floor of her apartment building. The note she left explained she killed herself because she was lonely.

A reporter interviewed the woman's neighbor, who said, "I wish I'd known she was lonesome. I'm lonesome myself."

Here were two lonely people who lived next door to each other, yet never bothered to say, "Hello." Does that suggest something to y'all?

To the question Elvis sang about, "Are you lonesome tonight?" — there is no need to be. By believing and putting our faith in God, we can enjoy God's presence and friendship.

By asking Jesus Christ to fill your life with His presence, and by attending one of His churches, you can beat loneliness.

See you in church.
Brother Poor

Prayer by Mrs. Poor:

Show us the wisdom, O Lord, of being a good neighbor. Amen.

A LITTLE PRAYER ROCK

I'm your little prayer rock . . .
    and this is what I'll do.
Just put me on your pillow
    till the day is through.
Then turn back the covers
    and climb into your bed
And Whack!
Your little prayer rock
    will hit you on your head.
Then you will remember –
    now that the day is through,
To kneel and say your prayers
    as you know you should do.
Then when you are finished,
    just dump me on the floor.
I'll stay there through nighttime
    to give you help once more.
When you get up next morning,
    Clunk! I stub your toe
So you will remember
    your morning prayers
    before you go.
Then put me back
    upon your pillow
    when your bed is made

And your clever little prayer rock
will continue in your aid.
(source unknown)

Prayer by Mrs. Poor:

May we not have to hit our head or stub our toe to remember to talk with You, Lord. Amen.

'CEPT GOD

We sure did have quite a storm the other day. It rained so hard the ducks in our pond got under the bridge. And thunder and lightening — Wow! There sure was a lot of power being demonstrated that day.

It made us all think some, too. We think we're so big and all fired important. But when the lights go off, we not only find ourselves in the dark, we find ourselves somewhat frightened and dependent.

There's something most humbling about looking up into a dark, stormy sky that backgrounds brilliant forked lightening and acts as a sounding board for booming, shaking thunder. Reminds me of the two little boys who were playing. One said he was so tuff that he could lick anybody. The other little fella simply replied, "'Cept God." The bigger boy restated his position, "I said I could lick anybody." "'Cept God," came the response. "Alright, alright! I can lick anybody 'cept God." And they went happily on their way.

My Christian friends, as progressive 21st-century people, we can solve most of our personal problems. But sooner or later, as skies get dark, we tremble in our limitations, and we realize the truth in the little boy's words, "'Cept God." Amen.
Brother Poor

Prayer by Mrs. Poor:

O, Lord, our Lord, how majestic is Your name in all the earth! Help us to answer that question again raised in Psalm 8. Amen.

GOODBYE TO MRS. DELIA,
MY BELOVED MOTHER-IN-LAW

Mrs. Poor's mama passed away last week. She was 84 years young and was alert and sharp as a tack right up until the end. She never lost her wonderful sense of humor; and as usual, even on her deathbed, she got the last word — a very firm "Amen" to my prayer.

I was touched at how many people came out to show their respect and to speak with her family — young people as well as old, family and in-laws, friends and neighbors, locals and folks from Florida to Washington, D.C.

I loved the old girl, and she loved us all. She always enjoyed reading the many cards I've sent her over the 35 years I've known her. In her honor, here's my last mother-in-law joke. It's a true story.

My mother-in-law, who everyone called Mrs. Delia, never could drive too good. But that didn't stop her from occasionally taking the family truck and driving down the road a few miles to visit with another farm family.

Once when she was returning from such a visit, she must have been driving faster than she realized. When she tried to turn off the main road onto a dirt road that led to her farm, she missed the road, ran through a ditch, and knocked over a fence post.

When she came home, she told her husband about the bent fender. "Delia," he said, "it's a wonder you didn't kill yourself." "Well, I would have," Mrs. Delia said rather calmly, "if I hadn't been a good driver."

Goodbye, Mrs. Delia — thanks for the laughter, and the love, and the beautiful memories. Our loss is Heaven's gain! I look forward to laughing with you again in heaven some day.

Brother Poor

Prayer by Mrs. Poor:

Thank you, God, for caring Christian parents and thoughtful and loving in-laws. Amen.

GOD BLESS SUNDAY SCHOOL
TEACHERS

When Mrs. Poor asked me what I wanted for my birthday, I told her I thought I might like to go up to Lake Junaluska for a few days. She didn't seem too surprised; she knows how much I love that place.

We loaded up the old Toyota and headed up into them hills again. We sat in with a group of Sunday School teachers who had got together to study the upcoming International Lessons on the gospel of Luke. Dr. Evelyn Laycock was our teacher, and is she ever some kind of great! I learned a lot from her guidance, and I also learned a lot from the other members of our class — Sunday School teachers from North Carolina, South Carolina, Georgia, Florida, and Mississippi.

What stood out to me most was the joy these teachers had in their faces, and voices and eyes. They had a message about the love that God offers, the joy that Jesus gives, and the hope that the Christian faith promises. But as they told their personal stories, some of them had to pause a little to let the tears come.

Things like a son with Lou Gehrig's disease, or a son who had committed suicide, or the recent passing of a loved one, or a prodigal daughter.

Nevertheless, although the tears came – back of the tears was the joy of being in Christ. Dr. Laycock's comment: "The more you and I love, the more suffering we will have; however, the more you and I love, the more joy we will have! Tears are only liquid love," she said.

Dr. Laycock's final challenge: "Now go back to your local churches and teach good Sunday School lessons about the gospel of Luke. Teach about cocoons changing into butterflies, bulbs to flowers, sorrows to joy, and pain and death to living in Christ!"

This mountain-top experience concluded with these words from "The Hymn of Promise":

> In the bulb there is a flower;
> In the seed, an apple tree;
> In cocoons, a hidden promise:
> Butterflies will soon be free!

There's a dawn in every darkness,
Bringing hope to you and me;
In our death, a resurrection;
At the last, a victory . . .

There's a song in every silence,
Seeking word and melody;
There's a dawn in every darkness,
Bringing hope to you and me.

In our death, a resurrection,
At the last, a victory . . . Amen.

God bless our Sunday School teachers.

Brother Poor

Prayer by Mrs. Poor:

God bless our Sunday School teachers. Amen.

A MALE CHAUVINIST GENIE

Me and Mrs. Poor have been fussing some here lately. I've been on the road a lot this month; and frankly, I haven't helped much around the house. Besides, we also chose to help our children by giving them some extra money. So, when you're tired and short of money, it's easier to fuss at each other.

For those of you who wrongly think that true Christians don't fuss, you better re-read about ol' Hosea and Gomer. For the rest of you who also fuss a little every now and then, you might enjoy this story.

A married couple had a spat; and it was serious enough for the wife to storm out of the house to go to her mother's. As she hurried down the back steps, she nearly fell by tripping on something she'd never seen before — an Aladdin's lamp.

Well, we all know what to do with an Aladdin's lamp, don't we? She did, too, and sure 'nuf, out popped a Genie.

"I am at your command," the Genie said. "I will grant you three wishes for whatever you desire. Name it and it's yours. However, there's one catch that might be hard for you to live with — whatever you get, your husband will get twice as much."

Naturally, the wife wasn't too thrilled about her husband's good fortune, but you don't quibble with a generous Genie — even if he is a male chauvinist.

"First," she said, "I would like a million dollars." Poof! Just like that, a million dollars lay at her feet. She leaped for joy, but came down to earth again when she remembered that "ol' meanie" was in the house counting his two million.

The Genie asked for her second wish. "Next, I'd like a pile of diamonds three feet high." Poof! Again, right next to the money, appears a mound of sparkling diamonds a yard high.

"I don't mean to dampen your spirits," the Genie cautioned, "But your husband is sitting in his Lazy Boy recliner with a pile of diamonds on both sides, counting his money. So maybe you'd like to forgo your third and final wish?"

The wife thought about that a moment or two, but then said, "No, Genie, I'd like that one last wish. What i want you to do . . . is scare me half to death."

Brother Poor

Prayer by Mrs. Poor:

When we get tired and short of money, give us an extra dose of Jesus' kindness, O, Lord. Amen.

KING OF THE JUNGLE

Me and Mrs. Poor went to the zoo the other day, and did we ever have ourselves a good time. I like the monkeys and giraffes; and Mrs. Poor sorta goes for them zebras and elephants. We both enjoy the bears and the seals. Be sure to take your family to a zoo — it's a real fun thing to do.

I'm reminded of an animal story: "The lion came roaring through the jungle and called out to the zebra, "Hey, Stripes, get over here. Who's the king of the jungle?" he demanded.

"Why, you are," the zebra replied. "That's right," said the lion, "and don't you forget it."

The lion next called out to the giraffe: "Hey, Neck, do you know who is king of the jungle?"

"Yes, sir," the giraffe answered, "You are."

Feeling quite satisfied with himself, the lion strutted down to the water hole where the old elephant was taking his evening bath. Unfortunately, the elephant had had a bad day and was in a bad mood. He thought to himself, "I've had about enough of that loud-mouth lion. He better not come around here bothering me today."

Sure enough, here came Mr. Lion. "Hey, Ears," he called out, "who is king of the jungle?" With that, the elephant picked the lion up with his trunk, banged him on the ground several times, then threw him through the air and bounced him off a tree.

The lion got up, shook himself off, and said, "My goodness, you don't have to get so riled up about it just because you don't know the answer."

Now I've got a question for y'all. "Hey, reader, who is King of kings? Who made all the animals? Who made you and me?" And if you know the answer, then it is time that you answered this more important one: "Why? Why did God create us?" Answer that one and you've discovered the meaning of life.

Brother Poor

Prayer by Mrs. Poor:

Help us to realize, O Creator God, that we are created to respond to your prevenient love. Amen.

Even God's "Favored" Suffer Hardships

In Luke's gospel, the angel Gabriel tells Mary that she's "favored among women."(Luke 1:28) Then life proceeds to lay on her many hard times – she becomes pregnant out of wed-lock; she has to travel to a strange town during the last month of her pregnancy; she delivers the baby in a "barn," with no mid-wife; she has to flee to Egypt as a refugee. At 12, her son runs away — or rather, chooses to remain behind without telling her. At 33, she watches her son's execution between two thieves.

Make no mistake about it — to be "favored of God" does not mean you will be spared a life of hardship. Let us follow Mary's example and "Keep all these things and ponder them in our heart." And let us follow the advice she gave at that wedding: "Whatsoever my son says unto you, do it!" (Luke 2:19) (John 2:5)

May Jesus be a part of your family; and may your mother and/or spouse be "favored among women."

O yes – and on Joseph's behalf – according to the Deuteronomic Law of that time, Mary was to be stoned. However, Joseph chooses to break the engagement quietly. Later, when he understood more fully, he took Mary's hand in his and together they followed the dream.

The greatest compliment Jesus could give Joseph was to refer to our Creator-God as "Abba" — which means father, daddy.

Remember when the woman taken in adultery was brought before Jesus to be stoned and Jesus stooped down and wrote something with his finger in the sand. He might have written "Abba" — for under similar circumstances, Joseph could have had Mary stoned and Jesus would never have been born.

Thank God for Mary and Joseph — the wonderful parents God chose for Jesus. And thank God for committed, Christian parents today.

See you in church.
Brother Poor

Prayer by Mrs. Poor:

Thank you, God, for committed, Christian parents. Amen.

MOM'S SURGERY

As I write, I am sitting in a waiting room in the Carolina Medical Center in Charlotte. My mother has had heart failure, and there is fluid built up in her lungs. Her test results reveal two 95% blockages and one 70%. She's 79, and a diabetic.

I'm sitting here with Mrs. Poor, my wonderful wife of 35 years of marriage. I have the Gideon Bible on my lap, and I am reading from the 27th Psalm. For those of you who have shared similar circumstances, you know the helpless, worrisome feeling. As I read, the comfort of God blesses.

I have always felt David began writing the 27th Psalm when he was a young fellow: "No fear — afraid of nothing — affirming the Lord as his strength — his light and his salvation — and asking God to teach him His way." What a wonderful affirmation for a young person to make.

But I get the feeling that David adds verses 13 and 14 after many years of seeing "the goodness of the Lord in the land of the living." The singing king, who lost two of his sons in death, concludes his Psalm with words of experience. Words which take on new meaning to me as I sit in this hospital waiting room:

"Wait on the Lord, be of good courage, and He shall strengthen thine heart. Wait, I say, on the Lord!" (Psalm 27:13-14)

Keep the faith; keep on keeping on.

Brother Poor

Prayer by Mrs. Poor:

Also, Almighty God, remind Brother Poor's readers of Isaiah 40:31. Amen.

Out-law Friend

I returned to an area where me and Mrs. Poor had "pastored" before. It was good to visit old friends, and relatives and in-laws – and even an out-law or two.

Truth is, I'm not kidding about this out-law comment. When I learned of a friend who had gotten himself into a jam with the police, I asked him if I could help him out in any way?

I will never forget. He said to me, "Well, preacher, I thank you for coming by. But this is just a business matter. It don't have anything to do with religion."

His comment kinda floored me for a minute. Then I told him what I want to tell y'all — "If your religion doesn't have anything to do with your business, then you don't have any religion!" Religion is not something you put on like you do your Sunday clothes. True Christians don't just carry their Bibles to church to be seen toting them. True Christians let the Bible be seen in their lives Monday through Saturday by the way they live.

Brothers and sisters, let's just try to walk it as we talk it by keeping our religion in our business.
Brother Poor

Prayer by Mrs. Poor:

Help us to be seven-days-a-week Christians — not just Christians on the seventh day. Amen.

ACRONYM FOR THANKS

"T" — Theology is the study of God. To some degree, everybody does it, sooner or later. Most conclude there had to be a creator, but never experience the creating power of God's presence in their life. That's sad.

"H" — Heaven or Hell? If you believe in God, do you believe we were only created to exist for about 80 years on this earth, and then die and rot in the ground? How foolish! It's either foolish for you to believe that or foolish for God to have done that. There must be more than just these brief 80 years. H is for Hope of Heaven.

"A" — Awareness of God's power and presence can make a lot of difference in your life. This power and presence can become personal. It is not enough to pray: "Our Father, who art in heaven .. We must pray: "My Savior, who art with me in my earthly triumphs and tribulations."

"N" — Neighbors, friends, significant others. No one can love God and hate God's children. No one can love God and ignore our neighbor's needs. No one can love God and cheat and lie to and use their neighbor. No one can love God as father without loving our neighbors as brothers and sisters. No one.

"K" — Keep on keeping on!
When times get tough,
and friends get few;
When you get confused
and don't know what to do . . .
Then Keep on Keeping on . . .
Praise the Lord and sing a song!
Life's too short – so quickly gone.
So just keep the faith, and
Keep on Keeping on. Amen.

"S" — Sin, Savior, Salvation.   *Brother Poor*

Prayer by Mrs. Poor:

May we express our thanks giving by our thanks living. Amen.

SICK MEMBER IN HOSPITAL

His wife said he was really depressed. She asked me to visit him in his hospital room. Our visit went something like this . . . .

He said he'd never thought much about being in a hospital. Said he'd worked hard all his life, always paid his bills on time, and had managed to save a little nest egg for retirement. But now, after only eighteen days in the hospital, he was worried about paying his bills.

I said, "Well, really, Bob, what did you expect? Sickness comes to all of us sooner or later. Even to the man with the full barns."

"Preacher, I guess I just thought I'd wake up dead one of these days and it would be all over. It really never crossed my mind I'd wake up between life and death, unable to work , and unable to die."

"Bob, it's just a matter of adjustment, and priorities, and values," I suggested. "You and Mollie can live on a lot less. You've just got to cut back some and become more selective."

"I don't know, Preacher," he said. "I just don't know."

"Look, Bob," I said, "what matters in this old life is quality time, not quantity. Lord, old Methuselah lived to be 969. Jesus, on the other hand, died at 33. Yet Jesus did more living, more loving, more lifting in one year than Methuselah did in all 1000 of his.

"Here's the secret: count your blessings; and then look around and see who you can share them with. Stewardship means taking real good care of what God has loaned you, and even trying to improve it a little for the next users. Some folk love things and use people; the secret is to use things and to love people."

"The bottom line is, if you are not a good steward, you're not a good Christian. On the other hand, if you are a good Christian, then you know the peace of Jesus Christ . . . which is worth more than all our money can buy."

Bob took my hand and asked for prayer. I prayed that he and Mollie may become alive to Jesus' presence daily. I pray the same for you folks.

Brother Poor

Prayer by Mrs. Poor:

Help us to recognize our blessings and then to share them. Amen.

"CHRISTMAS MUSIC"

I have had a wonderful, worshipful Sunday. At eleven, I attended a Methodist church and heard their Christmas cantata. At three, a community choral group presented their sacred-classical-secular concert. It was exceptional.

At five, I worshiped with the members of the church I grew up in. Someone has said, you can't go home again — and that's a really profound statement when taken to its conclusion. I guess about as close as you can come is returning to your home church and sitting in the congregation where you sat as a child. As we sang Christmas carols today, it brought back many meaningful memories.

At seven, another Christmas cantata. Let's see — that's two different United Methodist churches, one Presbyterian and one Baptist church — making four worship services in all! Not bad for one Lord's day. And I enjoyed each service.

Music and singing do it for me. I would have loved to have been a shepherd on that hillside on that first Christmas night when the angelic chorus sang: "Glory to God in the highest, and on earth, peace among men (and women) of good will." Maybe someday!

In the meantime, take your family to the church of your choice and enjoy a special Christmas cantata. Perhaps you can still catch a presentation of Handel's "Messiah" and hear that wonderful musical affirmation: "And He shall reign forever and ever. Hallelujah!"

Brother Poor

Prayer by Mrs. Poor:

Help us to know that even if we cannot all sing like angels or preach like Paul — that we can, each in our own way, tell of the love of Jesus. Amen.

THE PLACE WHERE YOU STAND
IS HOLY GROUND

I sure do enjoy visiting at Lake Junaluska. Ever heard of it? It's a church camp up in the mountains near Asheville, North Carolina. And this time of year, with the trees in full color, it is pure beautiful up there. God has painted his leaves again, and anyone who can't see the majesty of his creation probably doesn't understand Moses' feelings as he "saw God" on Mt. Horeb. Not only was the bush burning in that story, but Moses' heart got set on fire, too.

Well, some of the sisters of the church I'm serving now got tired of my bragging on that spot and said they'd like to see it; and at a weak moment, I agreed to taking 'em. To my pleasure and surprise, we had a wonderful time.

The schedule included shopping and eating out and site-seeing and sampling homemade fudge and shopping and sampling chocolate cookie chess cake with whipped cream and ice cream on top – plus a little more shopping. But believe me, Mrs. Poor can handle that shopping part real good; and those girls joyfully kept up with her.

For devotion and Bible study each day, I taught about the Beatitudes from our Lord's Sermon on the Mount. I suggest that they just might be "hierarchical" — that's one of them fancy words that means "like a ladder." My idea is that we can't become a peace-maker, or be merciful (the top of the beatitude ladder), until we first mourn a little, or understand justice (at the bottom of the hierarchy). Incidentally, that's an original idea. I've never heard it suggested before.

What do you think? Could climbing the beatitudes be sorta like climbing a spiritual ladder, or say climbing up a mountain with God for a beautiful mountain-top experience — the higher you get, the happier you get, the more blessed you get! I'm experimenting with the idea. Join me.

The last roses of fall that I cut from my flower garden and gave to a sick sister; them apples we brought down the mountain to peel and eat ever so often; the beautiful memories; the pictural, colorful views still in our minds; the fellowship and spiritual growth we brought back with us — that's what it's like to be on top of the mountain and to sense the presence of God.

Listen, do you hear it? Pick up your Bible and read Exodus, chapter 3, and let God speak to you just as he did to Moses, "for the place on which you are standing is holy ground" — because "God is."

The "Great I am" has spoken, and all the world is aglow with burning bushes and autumn beauty. Look and listen! God is revealing Himself!

Enjoy!   *Brother Poor*

Prayer by Mrs. Poor:

Thank you, dear God, for Lake Junaluska.

WHEN IS A PARDON
NOT A PARDON?

Me and Mrs. Poor used to live in the big city of Atlanta, Georgia. On most Sunday nights, we would listen to the Rev. Charles Allen preach. He was a big ole tall country boy with lots of homey appeal, and one of the best preachers I have ever heard. Here's the part you will find hard to believe. After his message/invitation, we would usually have to stand in line to get a place at the altar to kneel and pray. Ain't that wonderful?

One of the stories he told us was about a man named George Wilson who had committed murder. He was tried and, since it was about 1830, sentenced to hang.

President Andrew Jackson sent him a pardon, but Mr. Wilson did a strange thing. He refused to accept the pardon. No one seemed to know what to do next. So the case was carried to the Supreme Court. Then Chief Justice John Marshall wrote the opinion. In it he said, "A pardon is a slip of paper, the value of which is determined by the acceptance of the person to be pardoned. If it is refused, it is no pardon. George Wilson must be hanged." And he was!

While hanging on the cross, after being sentenced to die, Jesus yelled out, "Father, forgive them, for they do not know what they are doing." Two other men were killed with him.   One accepted his pardon and one did not. And so it is!

Have you accepted God's pardon? By the way, today Jesus would probably call out: "Father, forgive them, ...even though they know what they are doing!"

Brother Poor

Prayer by Mrs. Poor:

May we accept Your forgiveness with appreciation; and then may we forgive those who have offended us. Amen.

THE ZOO WITH 20 CHILDREN

I helped chaperone twenty little kindergarten children last week. We took them down to Myrtle Beach to the Waccatee Zoo. We sure did have a fun time. We saw lions and camels and alligators and big snakes and my favorite, "Checo," the chimpanzee.

We rode on a bus, with singing and laughing and, to be sure, some pushing and shoving and hitting and crying; then more singing and laughing. It never ceases to amaze me how kids can be fussing one minute and then be the best of friends the next. We adults hold grudges for years; but we miss so much genuine pleasure by not forgiving and forgetting like the kids do.

The owner and developer of the zoo gave me the grand tour, right up to how many chickens the big cats eat daily, to how much an ostrich egg costs, to his plans for future expansions. He sure loves animals; and he enjoys sharing them with children. I introduced him to my twenty "five-year-olds" as the Zoo Keeper. Their eyes were big as saucers as they greeted him by all together saying, "Thank you, Mr. Zoo Keeper." Then I noticed his eyes; they got a little watery.

As he waved goodbye to the children, he said to me, "Brother Poor, that's what it's all about — sharing with the children some of God's animals that they don't see often." With those twenty happy kindergarteners, I add my voice of appreciation: "Thank you, Mr. Zoo Keeper."

If y'all are down Myrtle Beach way, be sure to check out the Waccatee Zoo out in Soccastee. You will love it. There's lots of entertainment at the beach, but nothing as cheap, clean and family oriented as the zoo.

There's the biggest rodent I've ever seen! There are sheep with four horns called Jacob's sheep, all kinds of birds nesting in the lake trees, a natural alligator-breeding area, tigers and buffalo and miniature horses, etc. And in case you take twenty kindergarteners, they've got clean restrooms and nice picnic areas.

See you in Church, and at the zoo.

Brother Poor

Thank You for creating all the different and wonderful animals for us to enjoy. Amen.

" CHOPSTICKS"

Y'all ever hear the name "Paderewski" before. He was one of them high-falutin piano players. In fact, he was one of the world's leading pianists. Anyways, here is the story:

At one of Paderewski's concerts, the crowd anxiously awaited his arrival. A nine-year-old boy grew impatient with all the waiting but was fascinated with the beautiful Steinway piano on the stage. As little boys have been known to do, he slipped away from his mother and found his way to the stage. Oblivious to the crowd in the concert hall, he sat down at the piano and began to play his favorite and only tune, "Chopsticks."

The crowd was stunned. Some laughed, but others cried out in anger, and some even yelled for the ushers to take him out. Backstage, Paderewski looked out to see what was going on and saw the young fellow sitting where he was soon to be. He quickly went out, took his seat beside the little boy, and began playing a beautiful counter harmony. The little fellow was confused at first, but then he really got with it after Paderewski assured the boy that he was doing great and that they could do it together.

Isn't that a beautiful example of what the Holy Spirit is all about? Though the music of our lives may be incomplete, He will help to make something beautiful out of it.

Like a sign I once saw on a wall of a hospital in Salisbury, North Carolina: "We do our best, God does the rest." Not a bad thought: "Let's just do our best, and trust God to do the rest."

See you in church, *Brother Poor*

Prayer by Mrs. Poor:

May we be co-creative with You, O Lord. Amen.

THE 51ST PSALM

Was Moses "temporarily insane" when he killed that Egyptian who was beating up on his kinsman. (Genesis 2:13-15) That's sorta like killing a doctor who does abortions — killing to stop killings. I don't think that washes.

And speaking of "washes," did **Bath**-sheba know that King David was peeping at her; and if so, did she take a little longer to bathe that evening? Then was old Dave justified? No way.

One more illustration from the Old Testament (Genesis 39:7-21). Would Joseph had been justified if he had gone to bed with that man's wife down in Egypt? After all, she was wanting to. And how about date rapers today — fellows who contend that even though she's saying no, she means yes! Again, no way.

The question comes down to: what would you do if you had a gun in your hand when you opened a door and discovered your spouse in bed with your best friend? Who would you shoot? Your spouse, your best friend, or yourself? And more to the point, whoever you shot, would you be "temporarily insane," in a brief reactive psychosis, or just getting revenge?

Instead of attacking that Egyptian, Moses could have spoken to the Egyptian in terms of right and wrong. And Joseph was right. On the other hand, as the prophet Nathan points out most dramatically (II Samuel 12), David committed adultery and premeditated murder.

Later, a repentant King David wrote out his confession in the 51st Psalm. We all need to read that Psalm 51, and to re-read it frequently. In the meantime, let's all keep trying to work out our differences using Jesus' advice: "Do unto others as you would have others do unto you."

Brother Poor

Prayer by Mrs. Poor:

Create in us clean hearts, O God, and put a new and right spirit within us. Restore to us the joy of Thy salvation. (Psalm 51)

REV. D. O. LITTLE

Rev. D.O. Little, who pastors in too many churches, sure has got his people stirred up here lately. Seems a lot of members think he is living up to his name too good.

You see, Brother D. O. Little has decided not to offer Sunday night services 'cause not enough people were coming out to hear him preach. That is also his excuse for calling off Wednesday Bible studies and prayer meetings. I sure am glad that Jesus didn't feel that way – for most of the time he only had about twelve to hear him. Remember?

Neither does Rev. Little bother to visit much anymore; that is, unless you get sick or die. 'Course, he calls on newcomers and visitors until he "takes them in." Then he gets "too busy" to come around anymore.

Well, last week the choir director phoned in sick. Since her assistant was out of town, she asked the preacher to find a substitute until she could get over the flu-bug. Instead, he showed up

130

at choir practice and told them that he had decided to play a tape of some choral music next Sunday. Sister Susan, who usually sings a real sweet, soft soprano, spoke out quite loudly. "Okay, we can play some taped music, but we can also play a taped sermon, by George."

Well, I hope ole Brother D. O. Little gets this message. There are too many preachers who do not have the "nerve to serve" or the "love to visit," who still "flop to the top" and move on to bigger churches. May Brother D. O. Little, and preachers like him, realize that not everybody they meet are "taken in."

To me, the flip side of "get up and preach" is "get out and visit." The preacher has his say on Sunday mornings; he needs to get around and listen to what his congregation says Monday through Saturday. May all D. O. Littles get mad at this story and get more serious about the Lord's business. Like you preachers say, "If the shoe fits, wear it."   *Brother Poor*

131

Prayer by Mrs. Poor:

May the Rev. D. O. Littles be converted into Rev. D. O. Lots. Amen.

THANKS, LADIES

He was a regular attender at the local synagogue: a Pharisee, sorta like a trustee or a deacon of a protestant church today. He invited Jesus to his home to eat a meal with him after services. I've often wondered why? (See Luke 7:36-50.)

You see, in that day and time, about 30 A.D., it was customary to greet a guest with a kiss of peace. Not on the mouth, of course, but sorta like the French still do today. It was about like a handshake to us. It was just a custom, a courtesy greeting. But Simon, the Pharisee, the good church member, the deacon, did not greet Jesus courteously. Wonder why not?

Also, because the streets were dirty and sandals were worn and left at the door, cool water was poured over the guest's feet, both to cleanse and to comfort. No one extended this courtesy to Jesus. Why not, I wonder?

Further, let me point out that people back then did not sit at a table as we do to eat. Rather, they lay on a little low couch, propped up on their left elbow, and used their right hand to serve themselves. Their feet would be stretched out behind them, explaining how this woman's tears could have caused noticeable spots on Jesus' dirty feet.

Oh, yes, strange as this may seem to us today, since there were no televisions for entertainment, it was their custom to visit more and particularly if someone in the village was entertaining a guest. Friends, neighbors, even strangers would be free to drop in and stand around the outer walls of the courtyard where the meal was being served.

One final point about first-century Jewish customs. Traditional women in the East still keep their bodies hidden in long dress and veils. They do not show or let down their hair in public. It was shocking to Simon that this sinful woman of the street let down her hair and wiped Jesus' feet and kissed them.

It was also pretty shocking for that first-century society for Jesus to treat women with worth and respect and equality. No wonder the women wept when Jesus carried his cross by them (Luke 23:27-28). This was incredibly revolutionary. When before had any Rabbi included women among his disciples?

And finally (that's the word most sermon hearers listen for), who was the first person Jesus appeared to after the resurrection? That's right . . . a woman. According to the Gospel of John, Mary Magdalene. And where was old Simon on that first Easter Son-rise morning? I wonder. I'll bet he was in a nice, comfortable bed somewhere sleeping. I wonder where he is today?

Thank you, women, for all that you do for the church. Jesus knows and appreciates your thoughtfulness. God bless you, *Brother Poor*

Prayer by Mrs. Poor:

Thank you for Jesus' example of elevating man's respect and expectation of women. Amen.

CUP OVERFLOWED

I spoke to the men of a church over in Whiteville this past week. Before I addressed them in the name of Jesus, one of the fellows gave a brief devotional. In his talk, he read the following poem. I liked it a lot, so I'm passing it on. Hope it lifts your spirits as it did mine . . . .

I've never made a fortune,
and I'll never make one now;
But it really doesn't matter
'cause I'm happy anyhow.
As I go along my journey,
I'm reaping better
than I've sowed,
I'm drinking from the saucer
'cause my cup has overflowed.

We don't have a lot of riches
and sometimes the going's tough;
But while we've got our kids
to love us,
I think we're rich enough.
I'll just thank God for my blessings

that His mercy has bestowed,
For I'm drinking from the saucer
'cause my cup has overflowed.

If he gives me strength and courage
when the way grows steep and rough,
I'll not ask for other blessings.
I'm already blessed enough.
May I never be too busy
to help bear another's load.
Then I'll be drinking from the saucer
'cause my cup has overflowed.

This poem reminds me of the 23rd Psalm . . . "My cup runneth over!"

See you in church.
Brother Poor

Prayer by Mrs. Poor:

With grateful hearts, O Lord, we realize that we are indeed drinking from the saucer. Amen.

MISSION TRIP

Me and Mrs. Poor have been getting some slack lately 'bout our mission-work trip to the Virgin Isles. Seems some people don't believe in missionary work. Sister Evelyn says there are some sinners within sight of the church who ain't saved yet; and besides, if I want to do some hard work for a change, then I can come to her house and paint anytime I want to.

Now, the good sister has got a point: "If you don't work and witness for Jesus at home — there ain't no need to go off somewheres else and try to do it there."

But, on the other hand, Christian believers ought to work and witness wherever they are led — and to do so as if it wuz their last opportunity.

Guess the idea is to just 'bloom' wherever you happen to get planted. Keep the faith, brothers and sisters, and continue to work and to witness for our Christ wherever and whenever you get the chance.

See you in church, *Brother Poor*

Prayer by Mrs. Poor:

Wherever you lead us, O Lord, may we be good witnesses. Amen.

HYPOCRITE MONEY

Once when me and Mrs. Poor was pastoring over in the Greenville area of our fine state, one of our members got caught trafficking in "homemade" twenty dollar bills. Funny thing is, he was ushering that month, and we were still having a hard time meeting our budget. Seems my member-usher was not only crooked, he was just as "tight" as some of our other members.

Oh well, since this was the onliest real bad thing I knew on him, I stood by him in court as a character witness. "His Honor" sentenced him to serve seven years in the Atlanta big house. After that, no one over in that area ever asked me to character witness again!

Now don't misunderstand me – I believe that if you do the crime, you should pull the time. But I also believe in conviction and CONVERSION, repentance and REDEMPTION, rebirth and REHABILITATION. I believe in a God who does not give up on us, even when we give up on ourselves. The God I know through Jesus Christ loves, forgives, and encourages us to try again, and again.

Brother Poor

Prayer by Mrs. Poor:

Thank you, Lord, for forgiving my sins. May I be as forgiving to others as You are to me. When I hear some real bad gossip, may I remember: '. . . there, save for the grace of God, am I . . . .' Amen.

PARAKEET

Chirpy the parakeet never saw what hit him. One minute, he was peacefully perched in his cage. The next, he was sucked in, washed off, and blown over.

The problem began when Chirpy's owner decided to clean Chirpy's cage with a vacuum cleaner. She removed the attachment from the end of the hose and stuck it in the cage. The phone rang, and she turned to pick it up. She'd barely said "hello" when "sssopp!" Chirpy got sucked in.

The bird owner gasped, put down the phone, turned off the vacuum cleaner, and opened the bag. There was Chirpy – still alive, but stunned.

Since the bird was covered in dust and dirt, she grabbed him and raced to the bath-room, turned on the faucet, and held Chirpy under the running water. Then, realizing that Chirpy was soaked and shivering, she did what any compassionate bird owner would do – she reached for the hair dryer and blasted the pet with hot air.

As you might imagine . . . Chirpy doesn't seem to sing as much these days – he just sits and stares a lot.

Can you relate to Chirpy? Most of us can. One minute you're seated in familiar territory with a song on your lips, then . . . The doctor calls. The divorce papers are served. The check bounces. A policeman knocks on your door. Somewhere in the trauma, you lose your joy — at least temporarily you forget the words to the song.

If Chirpy's story is your story, I recommend that you read a copy of a book which a friend gave me for Christmas. It's entitled "In the Eye of the Storm," and today's illustration came from it.

The author of this book, Max Lucado, is one of us. He is convinced that Jesus' tomb is empty, that His promise is not, and that the Easter sunrise will never fade.

See you folks in church,

Brother Poor

Prayer by Mrs. Poor:

When we forget the words of the song, help us to hum along until they come back to us. For they will. Amen.

WISE MEN AND WOMEN

This story comes from a sign out on I-95 which reads: "Wise Men Still Seek Him." Turn to your Bible and read Matthew, chapter 2, about the Wise Men.

Point No. 1 — If all the Zorastor priests had done was to see the Star in the sky, they never woulda found Jesus. They had to follow the Light; and so do we today.

Point No. 2 — The very first thing the Magi did when they discovered Jesus was to worship Him and to give. The two best reasons for going to church are still to worship and to give.

Point No. 3 — After the Wise Men knelt before Jesus, they went back home a different way. And so must we — After Christ is born in our life — we change. Remember, wise men and women still seek Him daily.

See you in church, *Brother Poor*

Prayer by Mrs. Poor:

Help us to follow the Light, O Lord, and not just to understand it. Amen.

DENOMINATIONS ARE LIKE CARS

We sure did have a mighty fine Thanksgiving worship over our way. Why, Methodists and Baptists came from all over to sing and pray and give thanks . . . and we had a great time together.

Someone said we just ought to combine; in fact, one person vowed as to how she didn't see no sense in different denominations. "We're all trying to get to the same place anyhow!" she said.

So I told her about my old green Buick. Using her line of reasoning, we ought to all be driving one. And put Havoline oil in it, and fill it up with some of that cheap gasoline at the Etna place.

How come some people drive Fords and others Hondas? How come there is a different gas station on every corner? The same reason there's a different denominational church on about every other corner.

We are different. We have different backgrounds, different cultures, different likes and dislikes. Some people like to shout, others would be scared to death if someone said "Amen" in their service. Some congregations all pray out loud at the same time; others sit and wait for the Spirit to move them — Quaker style. Some worshipers start at the back of their hymnals and read to the front in Hebrew. Some still conduct the Lord's Supper in Latin. Some prefer to go all the way under the water when they join; others just get sprinkled. Some insist on the old King James version, and the differences go on.

Seems to me the good Lord has made us all different. In fact, my three children are as different as night and day. The important thing is that I love them; and they love me; and that they love each other.

In church business, the important thing is that we feel loved, and experience our heavenly Father's guidance, and can work together as brothers and sisters of the faith.

Enjoy the church of your choice, and may God bless you. Amen. *Brother Poor*

Prayer by Mrs. Poor:

When we sometimes feel that we have the only way, forgive us for not respecting each other's preferences. Amen.

ALEXANDER THE GREAT

There's a story told about ole Alexander the Great that I appreciate. Seems the young conqueror was sitting on his throne judging. A young man was brought before the ruler on the charge of desertion — the penalty of death.

Even though the Great Alexander could not stand cowardliness, it was obvious that he was attracted to this young fellow who had fled during a time of battle.

"Son, what is your name?" he asked.

"My name is Alexander," replied the repentant soldier.

So Alexander judged: "I forgive you of your offense; but in the future, you must either change your behavior or change your name."

It seems to me there is a message here for those of us who have been forgiven by God and who call ourselves Christians, yet are still "cowards" in our witnessing and in our war against sin.

See you in Church!
Brother Poor

Prayer by Mrs. Poor:

May we who are known as Christians become more Christ-like. Amen.

GRAVESIDE SERVICE

I went to a funeral service the other day that was held out in the cemetery. They called it a graveside service.

Some real nice things were said over the deceased. Someone remembered that when Mr. Earl ran an oil and coal business, quite often he would give some needy family a load of coal or a delivery of oil during a hard winter. He never mentioned it, just gave it and seemed grateful to have it to give.

Another thing that was said that I liked was that the family and friends and relatives who were standing by the casket could have "hope" because our departed brother believed in the faith. That is, he had taken Jesus at his word in John 11:25 when He said, "I am the resurrection and the Life; he who believes in me, even though he die, yet shall he live, and whoever lives and believes in me shall never die."

Brothers and sisters of the faith, let us hold to that "hope," and in the meantime, let's give a few bags of coal. Hope and help go hand in hand in the Christian faith.

See you in church.
Brother Poor

Prayer by Mrs. Poor:

May our help offer hope. Amen

DESERT PETE

One of the best sermons I have ever read was written by old Desert Pete. He used a stub of a pencil on two sheets of wrapping paper, then placed it in a can for protection.

Next he wired the can to an old pump that was the onliest source of water along a lonely trail in this desert out West. Here's what he wrote:

This pump is all right as of June, 1932. I put a new sucker washer into it and it ought to last about five years. But the washer dries out and the pump has got to be primed. Under the white rock I buried a bottle with enough water in it to prime the pump — but not if you drink some first. First, prime the pump.

Pour about one-fourth and let her soak to wet the leather. Then pour in the rest medium fast and pump like heck. You'll git water. The well has never run dry. Just have faith. When you git watered up, fill the bottle and put it back like you found it for the next feller. Desert Pete

P.S. Don't go drinkin' none first. Prime the pump with it and you'll git all you can hold. And remember, life is like this pump. It has to be primed. I've given my last dime away a dozen times to prime my pump – and I've fed my last bean to a stranger. You got to git your heart fixed to give before you can be give to.

At times, I feel like there are too many people out there who would drink the water from the bottle first and to heck with the next person who passes by.

May God bless you if your heart has been fixed to give. And when the hard times come, and they usually do, sooner or later, remember old Desert Pete and his advice and just "pour medium fast and pump like heck."

Brother Poor

Prayer by Mrs. Poor:

Show us the wisdom, Lord, of priming our own spiritual pumps first, before we try to offer a cup of cold water in Your name. Amen.

DISCIPLESHIP REQUIRES FOCUS

A few years ago, Mike Carson was the student associate at the First Baptist Church over in Orum.

Well, he preached a revival in Whiteville a couple of weeks ago; and did he ever do a good job for our Lord.

The Reverend Dr. Michael Carter, later the chairman and Tyner professor of Religion and Philosophy at Emory University, told us a delightful story that happened to him once when he was preaching in another revival.

Seems this good sister of the church had some reservations about a college professor coming to her church to preach.

She felt he might be just preaching some of them airplane sermons. You know, the kind that go right over your head.

After Dr. Carter had preached three sermons into the revival, the good sister jolted him with this compliment, or at least, Mike thinks it was meant to be a compliment.

"Dr. Mike," she said, "I don't mind telling you that I was somewhat worried when I heard you were going to be our revival preacher. But I'm OK now, 'cause you've preached just like you don't have any education at all."

When we all got through laughing, Dr. Carter proceeded to tell us how we should be modern day disciples by focusing on faithfulness, obedience and spirituality.

Thanks, Dr. Mike, for not letting your education go over our heads.

Brother Poor

Prayer by Mrs. Poor:

Lord, enable our preachers to share the deeper thoughts in the Bible in a simple, meaningful manner. Amen.

JESUS' BLOOD

A ten-year-old little girl had an unusually peculiar blood disease. In order to live, she needed a special transfusion. Her younger brother had the same blood type, and could give her some of his life sustaining blood, if he would. His parents explained the situation to the little fellow, telling him how his sister needed his blood to live. He thought about it for a while, and then said, "OK, I'll do it."

After the hospital drew his blood, tears began to well up in his eyes. He asked his mother how long it would be before he died.

"You are not going to die," she said. Then she realized that her son thought if he gave his blood to his sister, she would live, but he would die. He was willing to die, so his sister might live.

That's a beautiful story of a child's love for his sister. But isn't that exactly what Jesus has done for us? Help us to understand how the Gospel writers placed the death of Jesus into the Jewish ritual of the Day of Atonement. Hence, thanks be to God for His unspeakable gift. *Brother Poor*

Prayer by Mrs. Poor:

Thanks be to Thee, Almighty Father, for Your love revealed through Christ. Amen.

TWO MONKS

Two Japanese monks were traveling down a wet, muddy road. Around a bend in the road, they met a lovely girl in a flowing silk kimono, unable to cross the intersection.

One monk immediately took the girl in his arms and carried her through the mud and onto dry ground. The monks continued their hike in silence until they reached their temple lodging that night. Then the monk who did not carry the girl could restrain himself no longer.

"We monks never go near females," he said, "most particularly, not young and pretty ones. That's dangerous and tempting. Why did you do it?"

"It was really no problem for me," the Sir Walter Raleigh-type monk replied. "You see, I left the girl back there, while you still seem to be carrying her."

Brother Poor

Prayer by Mrs. Poor:

Help us to turn loose of our unholy thoughts, O Lord, and to let You fill our minds with Christ-like thoughts. Amen.

NO BRAKES IN MOUNTAINS

Me and Mrs. Poor just got back from Pigeon Forge, Tennessee, the home of "Dollywood!"

And are they country up there or what? And am I right when I say "up there"? What beautiful mountains. I'm talking about God's majestic Great Smoky Mountains – miles and miles of Blue Ridge Parkway with steep hills, fallen rocks, ultra-sharp curves and down-grades of 45 degrees or more.

And guess what happened to us! Our brakes went out just when we were about to start down from Clingman's Dome. Talk about scary! I just wish ole James Moony, my black preacher buddy from Lumberton had been with me this time. He'd a turned white for sure.

But I learned a valuable lesson on this trip. Don't ride your brakes in the mountains – gear down instead. And I think maybe there's a moral here, too. Don't go speeding through life trying to get to Dollywood, or Hollywood, or even to Heaven, my Christian friends. You can travel so fast that you miss the beauty of the journey.

Instead, gear down and look over the ridges and enjoy the mountain flowers. Those fiery mountain bushes that Moses saw are still there for those of us who take time to smell the roses.

Brother Poor

Prayer by Mrs. Poor:

Grant us the insight to smell the roses and to enjoy Your beautiful world. Amen.

LIFE HAS ITS UPS
AND ITS DOWNS

When Jesus was baptized by John in the River Jordan, He felt the assurance that God was pleased with His life. What a wonderful feeling that must have been. (Luke 3:21-22)

But notice, instead of Jesus going into Jerusalem and preaching in the temple and saving thousands, He was led by the Holy Spirit into the "wilderness." Isn't that just the way life is — it has its ups and downs — its highs and lows.

In the wilderness, Jesus responded to temptation with a Scripture reference. Three times he said, "It is written," and quoted from the book of Dew-ter-ron-a-me, er — Due-ter-om-a-knee — Oh, well, you folks know which book I'm talking about. (Luke 4:1-13)

Then after the wilderness experience, Jesus went into the synagogue "as was His custom."
(Luke 4:14-30)

In following Jesus' example of being prepared to face temptation, we should:

1. Strive to feel God's acceptance;

2. Read and memorize Scripture;

3. Attend the church of our choice regularly.

> See you in church.
> *Brother Poor*

Prayer by Mrs. Poor:

Help us to know our scriptures better so that when we are tempted, we can respond like Jesus did, "It is written." Amen.

WHAT SHALT WE DO?

Here are ten commandments that a lot of people are following today:

Thou shalt have a good day!
Thou shalt enjoy lots of good, high-cholesterol foods.
Thou shalt watch lots of prime-time television.

Thou shalt have some good snacks ready for in-between TV shows.

Thou shalt shop often — charging, of course.

Thou shalt eat out often — it's a great way to keep a clean kitchen.

Thou shalt express yourself — whether it hurts others' feelings or not – just as long as you tell what you think is the truth.

Thou shalt give your children lots of money.

Thou shalt not pry into your children's affairs — just assume they are doing the right thing.

Thou shalt not abstain from having a few sexual encounters — for everyone else is doing it.

Here are some other choices to consider. Compare and contrast these commandments:

Thou shalt look around you and try to find someone to help every day.

Thou shalt exercise daily.

Thou shalt intentionally turn off the television and read something from the Bible, Sunday school lesson, etc.

Thou shalt do unto others as you would have others do unto you — but thou shalt do unto them first.

Thou shalt practice good stewardship — with ecological consideration for the next generation.

Thou shalt make all the money you can, save all the money you can, give all the money you can.

Thou shalt say and do the loving thing.

Thou shalt let your children earn an allowance.

Thou shalt talk with and listen to thy children often.

Thou shalt not risk getting or giving AIDS.

Now, here's my idea: if you are obeying more of the commandments from the first list than from the second, then you need to change your lifestyle and your value system. Better get to the church of your choice soon and regularly.   *Brother Poor*

Prayer by Mrs. Poor:

May we understand that the Ten Commandments are not a multiple choice test; but that all ten are a true/false test of our faithfulness. Amen.

SPRING IS CALLING ATTENTION TO THE RESURRECTION

The good Lord has given me and Mrs. Poor three children.

One has jumped out of airplanes; another sings like an angel; and the third has been in a movie. A paratrooper, a singer, and a movie star? Each different as night and day, but each loved dearly by their parents.

Now, ain't that the way it's 'posed to be — all God's children are different — different talents, different colors, different IQs, different beliefs. But red, yellow, black or white — we are all precious in His sight. He loves us all! He invites us all to live and love and serve with Him forever.

Take notice of the dogwoods and azaleas — the tulips springing up — the daffodils in their golden yellow — the multi-colored pansies — the rosebuds bursting open — all of nature is calling attention to the Resurrection! See you at the "Sonrise" service.

Brother Poor

Prayer by Mrs. Poor:

May we see that the season of Spring calls attention to the Resurrection event. Amen.

THE ABCs OF THE
CHRISTIAN FAITH

I couldn't think of a story to tell y'all today — so I just wrote out a sentence for every letter of the alphabet. Let's call it the ABCs of the Christian faith. Hope the good Lord gives you a blessing as you read it.

Always seek to know God's will and way for your life.

Believe on the Lord Jesus Christ.

Come before His presence often.

Develop a Christ-o-centric lifestyle.

Enter into His church with praise.

Forgive others as you expect God to forgive you.

Go forward each day with newness of faith.

Help someone or someone(s) daily.

Include recreation and relaxation in your busy schedule.

Join a Bible study or some support group and participate actively.

Keep an intercessory prayer list.

Love is the key word to happiness.

Make spiritual maturity your goal.

Never think "never!" Always leave room for hope!

Open your life to God's guidance.

Praying is an acquired skill. It is a method of focusing on God and thereby elevating our spirit. Pray often!

Quiet time daily is essential and worthwhile.

Represent your beliefs with proper behavior.

Stop putting things off that you know you should be doing.

Try to tithe your income – or at least be generous with what God gives you.

Unless you feel led to seek a change, support your minister and your church's program.

Visit the sick and the shut-ins, even when you don't feel like it. The blessing will be yours.

When you get sick, remember your blessings and former good times.

"X"mas is a poor way to spell "Christ"mas.

You should live each day as if it were your last

Zip your mouth when you feel like complaining – If you can't say something good, just shut up! On the other hand, when you feel like giving a compliment, speak up!

Now, here's a shorter form of the ABC's of the Christian faith: "Always **Be** Christ-like!"

See you in church.
Brother Poor

Prayer by Mrs. Poor:

*Indeed, O Lord, may we strive to Always **Be** Christ-like. Amen.*

MANY FORGET THAT GOD
SEES ALL MEN AS EQUAL

Captain John Newton sailed his crew to Africa, bought and/or captured slaves, barely kept the stronger ones alive via the crowded sea voyage back to America; and then, divided up the families by selling the slaves to "good ole Southern boys." Whites like to think their ancestors treated their slaves kindly, but the truth be known – most whites beat, raped and violated the cultural "roots" of Afro-Americans. Thank God, those days are "Gone With The Wind."

As for John Newton, he was converted. Just as Paul stopped persecuting the early Christians, Rev. Newton became an anti-slavery proponent. He wrote the hymn, "Amazing Grace." Remember the words:

> Amazing Grace
> How sweet the sound
> That saved a wretch like me.
> I once was lost,
> But now am found,
> Was blind, but now I see.
> (John 9:25)

Last week's Sunday school lesson was about a man blind from birth. But it seems to me he's not the onliest blind person in Chapter 9 of John's Gospel. This story concerns a form of blindness that even those with 20/20 vision can experience. For instance, if someone is out of work and has fallen on hard times, we tend to conclude that the person is lazy, dishonest and dangerous.

Conversely, we usually think of rich people as receiving God's blessings. Well, let me tell you – I know a lot of rich folk who are heading straight to hell; and a lot of poor folk who are heaven bound.

We Christians must not only become color blind, we must also realize that the ground at the foot of the cross is level.

Hope to see you in church.
Brother Poor

Prayer by Mrs. Poor:

Shower us with that Powerful Amazing Grace, O Lord, that converted Paul of Tarsus and Captain John Newton. Amen.

Too Close to Call

I like the story about the church softball game that was settling the championship. It was the game of the season and both churches had lots of rooters there.

The umpire was a local fellow who wanted to please both sides.

On a 3-2 pitch, the catcher shouted, "Yes, it had the corner. You're out!"

The batter yelled, "No way! It was outside. I'm walking."

The umpire thought about it for a few seconds and then turned around and shouted to the crowd: "Too close to call – tie ball! Throw it over."

I know how he felt, don't you? But, unfortunately, there are some calls we can't throw out. We have to make a decision.

Should both of us continue working or should one of us stay home with the child?

Can we afford that new house we want, or should we continue renting, or maybe buy a trailer home?

Should we continue this relationship? Perhaps, if we separate, we can find other mates who will please us more. Or should we remember how it used to be, and both try again to rebuild the friendship and trust and romance and mutual respect?

Some of the people we know have lovely homes, a cottage at the beach, two nice cars, and both have good jobs. And yet they don't seem to be happy. What is happiness?

According to Jesus, happiness is...

... Loving God with all your heart;

... Loving your neighbor as you do yourself;

... Loving yourself.

But the bottom line is... you can't love yourself if you don't know the love of God discovered through His prevenient grace, His forgiving grace, His redeeming grace.

The most important question is: "Have you accepted the gift of salvation in Jesus Christ?" I pray you settle that decision today.

It is too important to "throw out".

Brother Poor

Prayer by Mrs. Poor:

May we love You, Father God, with all of our mind, and our neighbor as ourselves. Amen.

Funeral of Teenager

One of the saddest, and hardest, things for a pastor to do is to preach a funeral of a young person who has died unexpectedly - like a teenager killed in a car accident.

The phone rings at 2 a.m., and you go to the home and weep with the parents. Of course, you don't have the words to explain "Why?" but if you're prayed up- and good preachers are most of the time - God helps you react to the situation.

At the funeral service, I tried to get across that God's intentional will isn't always possible because He has given us freedom to choose, and let's be honest, this old world doesn't always choose to do God's intended will. So, we must consider God's circumstantial will - which allows for accidents, evil, divorce, etc. But glory of glories, we can trust completely in God's ultimate will - for in the end - God's Will will be done. Amen.

I found an appropriate text in that part of the Christian Bible which we share with our Jewish friends, the Old Testament. In II Samuel 18:33, David has just gotten word that his son Absalom has been killed. He mourns: "O my son Absalom, my son, my son, Absalom! Would to God I had died for you. O Absalom, my son, my son!"

His mourning continues in Chapter 19, verse 4; but I kept reading because I knew the poet who penned Psalm Twenty-three would get it back together. And sure 'nuf, in Chapter 22, David sings again!

Listen to this composite: "The Lord is my rock, and my fortress, and my deliverer... In Him will I trust... The waves of death compassed me... in my distress I called upon the Lord... in the day of my calamity, the Lord was my stay... the Lord is my lamp, He lightens my darkness!"

At the death of a loved one, we mourn. But in time, with God's grace and the support of our friends, and because of our Christian faith, we sing again: "Praise God from whom all blessings flow!"

Brother Poor

Prayer by Mrs. Poor: Help us to sing joyfully the Doxology: "Praise God from whom all blessings flow."

Warts and All

Me and Mrs. Poor went to the movies the other day. We thought we'd enjoy seeing Snow White and those little fellows again. Besides, Mrs. Poor teaches kindergarten, and she knew her students would probably go see the film this summer.

But somehow or other, we got into the wrong show. We ain't never seen so much violence or heard such gosh awful language coming at us so quickly. It was a movie about a black fellow trying to survive in a big city. Believe you me, it weren't about no Snow White!

They had several different movies all playing at the same time, but we finally got set down in the right place to see "Snow White".

I could see my congregation represented in each one of them seven dwarfs: "Sleepy," who always dozes off during my sermons; "Grumpy," who I've come to discover is in every church; and of course, the preacher who couldn't even find the right movie was a good example of ole "Dopey".

About going into the wrong movie, I couldn't help but think maybe the good Lord was trying to tell me something about life - real life for a lot of unfortunate people who have to survive in some not too pleasant environments.

But all in all, even Snow White encounters the wicked, is lied to and deceived; and like Adam and Eve, she too bit into that apple.

In the fairy tales, when you kiss a frog, it can change into a handsome prince. In the real world, when you kiss a frog, you usually get warts

However, here is the joy: God loves us, warts and all! And though our sins be as scarlet, we can become "Snow White". (Isaiah 1:18)

In the meantime, let's just try to keep the faith! And good luck in finding the right movie. Looking forward to seeing you in church someday,

Brother Poor

Prayer by Mrs. Poor:

Thank you for loving us, O Lord, warts and all...

God Be With Ye!

Well, it's time for me and Mrs. Poor to say goodbye. We sure do hope that you folks have enjoyed reading about some of our good times and some of our hard times. Life ain't always easy, is it?

For fifty years, three children, and two grandchildren - me and Mrs. Poor have stuck together, worked together, and loved together. Yet I can remember the day I first met my wife as if it was just yesterday. It was a WOW!

And I can remember even better the second time I saw her. I was really looking forward to seeing her again. I searched the crowd, spotted her, and walked toward her. When our eyes met, I knew then that she was also looking for me. My heart started beating faster; and that was a double WOW!!

Fifty years later, Mrs. Poor can still make my old heart beat faster.

Someone recently asked Mrs. Poor if she'd ever thought about divorce. My wife said she'd never thought much about it 'cause we had agreed before God and witnesses "till death us do part," - through better or worse, richer or poorer, in sickness and in health. However, she said she had thought about murder a time or two.

Though I could never afford to give my wife that house she deserved, and though our children grew up and moved away geographically, and though our old bodies didn't stay young and fit - today we can look into each other's eyes, and holding hands, say harmoniously, "Rev. and Mrs. Poor are indeed **RICH!**

Thanks be to God for God's wonderful gift of love. May you know it, and may you share it.

Hope to see you all in church some day. If not in this world, perhaps in the next.

P.S. Did y'all know that the greeting "goodbye" is a shortened form of the old English phrase: **"God be with ye!"** And that is our final wish for each of you.... *Brother Poor*

The Final Prayer by Mrs. Poor

Dear Creator-creating God, whom we know in Christ to be loving, and healing, and encouraging, may Thy Kingdom come and Thy Will be done, on earth as it is in heaven. Amen. *Sister Poor*